MODERN BRITISH POETRY

EDITED BY
LOUIS UNTERMEYER

Author of "*Challenge*," "*Including Horace*,"
"*Modern American Poetry*," etc.

NEW YORK
HARCOURT, BRACE AND HOWE
1920

ACKNOWLEDGMENTS

FOR permission to reprint the material in this volume, the editor wishes, first of all, to acknowledge his debt to those poets whose co-operation has been of such assistance not only in finally determining upon the choice of their poems, but in collecting dates, biographical data, etc. Secondly, he wishes to thank the publishers, most of whom are holders of the copyrights. The latter indebtedness is specifically acknowledged to:

DOUBLEDAY, PAGE & COMPANY and A. P. WATT & SON—
For "The Return" from *The Five Nations* and for "An Astrologer's Song" from *Rewards and Fairies* by Rudyard Kipling. Thanks also are due to Mr. Kipling himself for personal permission to reprint these poems.

DOUBLEDAY, PAGE & COMPANY and MARTIN SECKER—
For the poem from *Collected Poems* by James Elroy Flecker.

E. P. DUTTON & COMPANY—
For the poems from *The Old Huntsman, Counter-Attack* and *Picture Show* by Siegfried Sassoon.

FOUR SEAS COMPANY—
For poems from *War and Love* by Richard Aldington and *The Mountainy Singer* by Seosamh MacCathmhaoil (Joseph Campbell).

HENRY HOLT AND COMPANY—
For poems from *Peacock Pie* and *The Listeners* by Walter de la Mare and *Poems* by Edward Thomas.

HOUGHTON MIFFLIN COMPANY—
For two poems from *Poems, 1908-1919*, by John Drinkwater, both of which are used by permission of, and by special arrangement with, Houghton Mifflin Company, the authorized publishers.

B. W. HUEBSCH—
For the selections from *Chamber Music* by James Joyce, *Songs to Save a Soul* and *Before Dawn* by Irene Ruther-

Acknowledgments

ford McLeod, *Amores, Look! We Have Come Through!*, and *New Poems* by D. H. Lawrence.

ALFRED A. KNOPF—

For poems from *The Collected Poems of William II. Davies, Fairies and Fusiliers* by Robert Graves, *The Queen of China and Other Poems* by Edward Shanks, and *Poems: First Series* by J. C. Squire.

JOHN LANE COMPANY—

For the selections from *Poems* by G. K. Chesterton, *Ballads and Songs* by John Davidson, *The Collected Poems of Rupert Brooke, Admirals All* by Henry Newbolt, *Herod* and *Lyrics and Dramas* by Stephen Phillips, *The Hope of the World and Other Poems* by William Watson, and *In Cap and Bells* by Owen Seaman.

THE LONDON MERCURY—

For "Going and Staying" by Thomas Hardy and "The House That Was" by Laurence Binyon.

THE MACMILLAN COMPANY—

For the selections from *Fires* and *Borderlands and Thoroughfares* by Wilfrid Wilson Gibson, *Poems* by Ralph Hodgson, the sonnet from *Good Friday and Other Poems* by John Masefield, and the passage (entitled in this volume "Rounding the Horn") from "Dauber" in *The Story of a Round-House* by John Masefield.

G. P. PUTNAM'S SONS—

For the title poem from *In Flanders Fields* by John McCrae.

THE POETRY BOOKSHOP (England)—

For two excerpts from *Strange Meetings* by Harold Monro and for the poems from the biennial anthologies, *Georgian Poetry*.

CHARLES SCRIBNER'S SONS—

For the quotations from *Poems* by William Ernest Henley.

FREDERICK A. STOKES COMPANY—

For the poem from *Ardours and Endurances* by Robert Nichols.

LONGMANS, GREEN & Co., as the representatives of B. H. BLACKWELL, of Oxford—

For a poem by Edith Sitwell from *The Mother*.

CONTENTS

Contents

Contents

v

Contents

Contents

Contents

viii

Contents

INTRODUCTORY

The New Influences and Tendencies

MERE statistics are untrustworthy; dates are even less dependable. But, to avoid hairsplitting, what we call "modern" English literature may be said to date from about 1885. A few writers who are decidedly "of the period" are, as a matter of strict chronology, somewhat earlier. But the chief tendencies may be divided into seven periods. They are (1) The decay of Victorianism and the growth of a purely decorative art, (2) The rise and decline of the Æsthetic Philosophy, (3) The muscular influence of Henley, (4) The Celtic revival in Ireland, (5) Rudyard Kipling and the ascendency of mechanism in art, (6) John Masefield and the return of the rhymed narrative, (7) The war and the appearance of "The Georgians." It may be interesting to trace these developments in somewhat greater detail.

THE END OF VICTORIANISM

The age commonly called Victorian came to an end about 1885. It was an age distinguished by many true idealists and many false ideals. It was, in spite of its notable artists, on an entirely different level from the epoch which had preceded it. Its poetry was, in the main, not universal but parochial; its romanticism was gilt and tinsel; its realism was as cheap as its showy glass pendants, red plush, parlor chromos and antimacassars. The period was full of a pessimistic resignation (the note popularized by Fitzgerald's Omar Khayyám) and a kind of cowardice or at least a negation which, refusing to see any glamour in the actual world, turned to the Middle Ages, King Arthur, the legend of Troy—to the suave surroundings of a dream-world instead of the hard contours of actual experience.

At its worst, it was a period of smugness, of placid and pious sentimentality—epitomized by the rhymed sermons of Martin Farquhar Tupper, whose *Proverbial Philosophy* was devoured with all its cloying and indigestible sweetmeats by thousands. The same tendency is apparent, though far less objectionably, in the moralizing lays of Lord Thomas Macaulay, in the theatrically emotionalized verses of Robert Buchanan, Edwin Arnold and Sir Lewis Morris—even in the lesser later work of Alfred Tennyson.

And, without Tupper's emptiness or absurdities, the outworn platitudes again find their constant lover in Alfred Austin, Tennyson's successor as poet laureate. Austin brought the laureateship, which had been held by poets like Ben Jonson, Dryden, Southey and Wordsworth, to an incredibly low level; he took the thinning stream of garrulous poetic conventionality, reduced it to the merest trickle—and diluted it.

The poets of a generation before this time were fired with such ideas as freedom, a deep and burning awe of nature, an insatiable hunger for truth in all its forms and manifestations. The characteristic poets of the Victorian

Introductory

Era, says Max Plowman, " wrote under the dominance of churchliness, of 'sweetness and light,' and a thousand lesser theories that have not truth but comfort for their end."

The revolt against this and the tawdriness of the period had already begun; the best of Victorianism can be found not in men who were typically Victorian, but in pioneers like Browning and writers like Swinburne, Rossetti, William Morris, who were completely out of sympathy with their time.

But it was Oscar Wilde who led the men of the now famous 'nineties toward an æsthetic freedom, to champion a beauty whose existence was its " own excuse for being." Wilde's was, in the most outspoken manner, the first use of æstheticism as a slogan; the battle-cry of the group was actually the now outworn but then revolutionary " Art for Art's sake "! And, so sick were people of the shoddy ornaments and drab ugliness of the immediate past, that the slogan won. At least, temporarily.

THE RISE AND DECLINE OF THE ÆSTHETIC PHILOSOPHY

The Yellow Book, the organ of a group of young writers and artists, appeared (1894-97), representing a reasoned and intellectual reaction, mainly suggested and influenced by the French. The group of contributors was a peculiarly mixed one with only one thing in common. And that was a conscious effort to repudiate the sugary airs and prim romantics of the Victorian Era.

Almost the first act of the " new " men was to rouse and outrage their immediate predecessors. This end-of-the-century desire to shock, which was so strong and natural an impulse, still has a place of its own—especially as an antidote, a harsh corrective. Mid-Victorian propriety and self-satisfaction crumbled under the swift and energetic audacities of the sensational younger authors and artists; the old walls fell; the public, once so apathetic to *belles lettres,* was more than attentive to every phase of literary experimentation. The last decade of the nineteenth century was so tolerant of novelty in art and ideas, that it would seem, says Holbrook Jackson in his penetrative summary, *The Eighteen-Nineties,* "as though the declining century wished to make amends for several decades of artistic monotony. It may indeed be something more than a coincidence that placed this decade at the close of a century, and *fin de siècle* may have been at once a swan song and a death-bed repentance."

But later on, the movement (if such it may be called), surfeited with its own excesses, fell into the mere poses of revolt; it degenerated into a half-hearted defense of artificialities.

It scarcely needed W. S. Gilbert (in *Patience*) or Robert Hichens (in *The Green Carnation*) to satirize its distorted attitudinizing. It strained itself to death; it became its own burlesque of the bizarre; an extravaganza of extravagance. "The period" (I am again quoting Holbrook Jackson) "was as certainly a period of decadence as it was a period of renaissance. The decadence was to be seen in a perverse and finicking glorification of the fine arts and mere artistic virtuosity on the one hand, and a militant commercial movement on the other. . . . The eroticism which became so prevalent in the verse of many of the younger poets was minor because it was little more than a pose—not because it was erotic. . . . It was a passing mood which gave the poetry of the hour a hothouse fragrance; a perfume faint yet unmistakable and strange."

But most of the elegant and disillusioned young men overshot their mark. Mere health reasserted itself; an inherent repressed vitality sought new channels. Arthur Symons deserted his hectic Muse, Richard Le Gallienne abandoned his preciosity, and the group began to disintegrate. The æsthetic philosophy was wearing thin; it had already begun to fray and reveal its essential shabbiness. Wilde himself possessed the three things which he said the English would never forgive—youth, power and enthusiasm. But in trying to make an exclusive cult of beauty, Wilde had also tried to make it evade actuality; he urged that art should not, in any sense, be a part of life but an escape from it. "The proper school to learn art in is not Life—but Art." And in the same essay ("The Decay of Lying") he wrote, "All bad Art comes from returning to Life and Nature, and elevating them into ideals." Elsewhere he said, "The first duty in life is to be as artificial as possible. What the second duty is no one has discovered."

Such a cynical and decadent philosophy could not go unchallenged. Its artistocratic blue-bloodedness was bound to arouse the red blood of common reality. This negative attitude received its answer in the work of that yea-sayer, W. E. Henley.

Introductory

WILLIAM ERNEST HENLEY

Henley repudiated this languid æstheticism; he scorned a negative art which was out of touch with the world. His was a large and sweeping affirmation. He felt that mere existence was glorious; life was coarse, difficult, often dangerous and dirty, but splendid at the heart. Art, he knew, could not be separated from the dreams and hungers of man; it could not flourish only on its own essences or technical accomplishments. To live, poetry would have to share the fears, angers, hopes and struggles of the prosaic world. And so Henley came like a swift salt breeze blowing through a perfumed and heavily-screened studio. He sang loudly (sometimes even too loudly) of the joy of living and the courage of the "unconquerable soul." He was a powerful influence not only as a poet but as a critic and editor. In the latter capacity he gathered about him such men as Robert Louis Stevenson, Rudyard Kipling, Thomas Hardy, H. G. Wells, W. B. Yeats, T. E. Brown, J. M. Barrie. None of these men were his disciples, but none of them came into contact with him without being influenced in some way by his sharp and positive personality. A pioneer and something of a prophet, he was one of the first to champion the paintings of Whistler and to proclaim the genius of the sculptor Rodin.

If at times Henley's verse is imperialistic, over-muscular and strident, his noisy moments are redeemed not only by his delicate lyrics but by his passionate enthusiasm for nobility in whatever cause it was joined. He never disdained the actual world in any of its moods—bus-drivers, hospital interiors, scrubwomen, a panting train, the squalor of London's alleys, all found a voice in his lines —and his later work contains more than a hint of the delight in science and machinery which was later to be sounded more fully in the work of Rudyard Kipling.

THE CELTIC REVIVAL AND J. M. SYNGE

In 1889, William Butler Yeats published his *Wanderings of Oisin;* in the same year Douglas Hyde, the scholar and folk-lorist, brought out his *Book of Gaelic Stories.*

The revival of Gaelic and the renascence of Irish literature may be said to date from the publication of those two books. The fundamental idea of both men and their followers was the same. It was to create a literature which would express the national consciousness of Ireland through a purely national art. They began to reflect the strange background of dreams, politics, suffering and heroism that is immortally Irish. This community of fellowship and aims is to be found in the varied but allied work of William Butler Yeats, " A. E." (George W. Russell), Moira O'Neill, Lionel Johnson, Katharine Tynan, Padraic Colum and others. The first fervor gone, a short period of dullness set in. After reanimating the old myths, surcharging the legendary heroes with a new significance, it seemed for a while that the movement would lose itself in a literary mysticism. But an increasing concern with the peasant, the migratory laborer, the tramp, followed; an interest that was something of a reaction against the influence of Yeats and his mystic other-worldliness. And, in 1904, the Celtic Revival reached its height with John Millington Synge, who was not only the greatest dramatist of the Irish Theatre, but (to quote such contrary critics as George Moore and Harold Williams) "one of the greatest dramatists who has written in English." Synge's poetry, brusque and all too small in quantity, was a minor occupation with him and yet the quality and power of it is unmistakable. Its content is never great but the raw vigor in it was to serve as a bold banner—a sort of a brilliant Jolly Roger —for the younger men of the following period. It was not only this dramatist's brief verses and his intensely musical prose but his sharp prefaces that were to exercise such an influence.

In the notable introduction to the *Playboy of the Western World,* Synge declared, "When I was writing *The Shadow of the Glen* some years ago, I got more aid than any learning could have given me from a chink in the floor of the old Wicklow house where I was staying, that let me hear what was being said by the servant girls in the kitchen. This matter is, I think, of some importance; for in countries where the imagination of the people, and the language they use, is rich and living, it is possible for a writer to be rich and copious in his words—and at the same time to give the reality which is at the root of all poetry, in a natural and comprehensive form." This quotation explains his idiom, possibly the sharpest-flavored and most vivid in modern literature.

As to Synge's poetic power, it is unquestionably greatest in his plays. In *The Well of the Saints, The Playboy of the Western World* and *Riders to the Sea* there are more poignance, beauty of form and richness of language than in any piece of dramatic writing since Elizabethan times. Yeats, when he first heard Synge's early one-act play, *The Shadow of the Glen,* is said to have exclaimed "Euripides." A half year later when Synge read him *Riders to the Sea,* Yeats again confined his enthusiasm to a single word:—"Æschylus!" Years have shown that Yeats's appreciation was not as exaggerated as many might suppose.

But although Synge's poetry was not his major concern, numbering only twenty-four original pieces and eighteen translations, it had a surprising effect upon his followers. It marked a point of departure, a reaction against both the too-polished and over-rhetorical verse of his immediate predecessors and the dehumanized mysticism of many of his associates. In that memorable preface to his *Poems* he wrote what was a slogan, a manifesto and at the same time a classic *credo* for all that we call the "new" poetry. "I have often thought," it begins, "that at the side of poetic diction, which everyone condemns, modern verse contains a great deal of poetic material, using 'poetic' in the same special sense. The poetry of exaltation will be always the highest; but when men lose their poetic feeling for ordinary life and cannot write poetry of ordinary things, their exalted poetry is likely to lose its strength of exaltation in the way that men cease to build beautiful churches when they have lost happiness in building shops. . . . Even if we grant that exalted poetry can be kept successfully by itself, the strong things of life are needed in poetry also, to show that what is exalted or tender is not made by feeble blood."

RUDYARD KIPLING

New tendencies are contagious. But they also disclose themselves simultaneously in places and people where there has been no point of contact. Even before Synge published his proofs of the keen poetry in everyday life, Kipling was illuminating, in a totally different manner, the wealth of poetic material in things hitherto regarded as too commonplace for poetry. Before literary England had quite recovered from its surfeit of Victorian priggishness and pre-Raphaelite delicacy, Kipling came along with high spirits and a great tide of life, sweeping all before him. An obscure Anglo-Indian journalist, the publication of his *Barrack-room Ballads* in 1892 brought him sudden notice. By 1895 he was internationally famous. Brushing over the pallid attempts to revive a pallid past, he rode triumphantly on a wave of buoyant and sometimes brutal joy in the present. Kipling gloried in the material world; he did more—he glorified it. He pierced the coarse exteriors of seemingly prosaic things—things like machinery, bridge-building, cockney soldiers, slang, steam, the dirty by-products of science (witness " M'Andrews Hymn " and " The Bell Buoy ")—and uncovered their hidden glamour. " Romance is gone," sighed most of his contemporaries,

" . . . and all unseen
Romance brought up the nine-fifteen."

Introductory

That sentence (from his poem " The King ") contains the key to the manner in which the author of *The Five Nations* helped to rejuvenate English verse.

Kipling, with his perception of ordinary people in terms of ordinary life, was one of the strongest links between the Wordsworth-Browning era and the latest apostles of vigor, beginning with Masefield. There are occasional and serious defects in Kipling's work—particularly in his more facile poetry; he falls into a journalistic ease that tends to turn into jingle; he is fond of a militaristic drum-banging that is as blatant as the insularity he condemns. But a burning, if sometimes too simple faith, shines through his achievements. His best work reveals an intensity that crystallizes into beauty what was originally tawdry, that lifts the vulgar and incidental to the place of the universal.

JOHN MASEFIELD

All art is a twofold revivifying—a recreation of subject and a reanimating of form. And poetry becomes perennially " new " by returning to the old—with a different consciousness, a greater awareness. In 1911, when art was again searching for novelty, John Masefield created something startling and new by going back to 1385 and *The Canterbury Pilgrims*. Employing both the Chaucerian model and a form similar to the practically forgotten Byronic stanza, Masefield wrote in rapid succession, *The Everlasting Mercy* (1911), *The Widow in the Bye Street* (1912), *Dauber* (1912), *The Daffodil Fields* (1913)—four astonishing rhymed narratives and four of the most remarkable poems of our generation. Expressive of every rugged phase of life, these poems, uniting old and new manners, responded to Synge's proclamation that " the strong things of life are needed in poetry also . . . and it may almost be said that before verse can be human again it must be brutal."

Masefield brought back to poetry that mixture of beauty and brutality which is its most human and enduring quality. He brought back that rich and almost vulgar vividness which is the very life-blood of Chaucer, of Shakespeare, of Burns, of Villon, of Heine—and of all those who were not only great artists but great humanists. As a purely descriptive poet, he can take his place with the masters of sea and landscape. As an imaginative realist, he showed those who were stumbling from one wild eccentricity to another to thrill them, that they themselves were wilder, stranger, far more thrilling than anything in the world—or out of it. Few things in contemporary poetry are as powerful as the regeneration of Saul Kane (in *The Everlasting Mercy*) or the story of *Dauber,* the tale of a tragic sea-voyage and a dreaming youth who wanted to be a painter. The vigorous description of rounding Cape Horn in the latter poem is superbly done, a masterpiece in itself. Masefield's later volumes are quieter in tone, more measured in technique; there is an almost religious ring to many of his Shakespearian sonnets. But the swinging surge is there, a passionate strength that leaps through all his work from *Salt Water Ballads* (1902) to *Reynard the Fox* (1919).

Introductory

"THE GEORGIANS" AND THE YOUNGER MEN

There is no sharp statistical line of demarcation between Masefield and the younger men. Although several of them owe much to him, most of the younger poets speak in accents of their own. W. W. Gibson had already reinforced the "return to actuality" by turning from his first preoccupation with shining knights, faultless queens, ladies in distress and all the paraphernalia of hackneyed mediæval romances, to write about ferrymen, berry-pickers, stone-cutters, farmers, printers, circus-men, carpenters—dramatizing (though sometimes theatricalizing) the primitive emotions of uncultured and ordinary people in *Livelihood, Daily Bread* and *Fires*. This intensity had been asking new questions. It found its answers in the war; repressed emotionalism discovered a new outlet. One hears its echoes in the younger poets like Siegfried Sassoon, with his poignant and unsparing poems of conflict; in Robert Graves, who reflects it in a lighter and more fantastic vein; in James Stephens, whose wild ingenuities are redolent of the soil. And it finds its corresponding opposite in the limpid and unperturbed loveliness of Ralph Hodgson; in the ghostly magic and the nursery-rhyme whimsicality of Walter de la Mare; in the quiet and delicate lyrics of W. H. Davies. Among the others, the brilliant G. K. Chesterton, the facile Alfred Noyes, the romantic Rupert Brooke (who owes less to Masefield and his immediate predecessors than he does to the passionately intellectual Donne), the introspective D. H. Lawrence and the versatile J. C.

Squire, are perhaps best known to American readers.

All of the poets mentioned in the foregoing paragraph (with the exception of Noyes) have formed themselves in a loose group called " The Georgians," and an anthology of their best work has appeared every two years since 1913. Masefield, Lascelles Abercrombie and John Drinkwater are also listed among the Georgian poets. When their first collection appeared in March, 1913, Henry Newbolt, a critic as well as poet, wrote: " These younger poets have no temptation to be false. They are not for making something ' pretty,' something up to the standard of professional patterns. . . . They write as grown men walk, each with his own unconscious stride and gesture. . . . In short, they express themselves and seem to steer without an effort between the dangers of innovation and reminiscence." The secret of this success, and for that matter, the success of the greater portion of English poetry, is not an exclusive discovery of the Georgian poets. It is their inheritance, derived from those predecessors who, " from Wordsworth and Coleridge onward, have worked for the assimilation of verse to the manner and accent of natural speech." In its adaptability no less than in its vigor, modern English poetry is true to its period—and its past.

This collection is obviously a companion volume to *Modern American Poetry*, which, in its restricted compass, attempted to act as an introduction to recent native verse. *Modern British Poetry* covers the same period (from about 1870 to 1920), follows the same chronological scheme, but it is more amplified and goes into far greater detail than its predecessor.

The two volumes, considered together, furnish interesting contrasts; they reveal certain similarities and certain strange differences. Broadly speaking, modern American verse is sharp, vigorously experimental; full of youth and its occasional—and natural—crudities. English verse is smoother, more matured and, molded by centuries of literature, richer in associations and surer in artistry. Where the American output is often rude, extremely varied and uncoördinated (being the expression of partly indigenous, partly naturalized and largely unassimilated ideas, emotions and races), the English product is formulated, precise and, in spite of its fluctuations, true to its past. It goes back to traditions as old as Chaucer (witness the narratives of Masefield and Gibson) or tendencies as classic as Drayton, Herrick and Blake—as in the frank lyrics of A. E. Housman, the artless lyricism of Ralph Hodgson, the naïf wonder of W. H. Davies. And if English poetry may be compared to a broad and luxuriating river (while American poetry might be described as a sudden rush of unconnected mountain torrents, valley streams and city sluices), it will be inspiring to observe how its course has been temporarily deflected in the last forty years; how it has swung away from one tendency toward another; and how, for all its bends and twists, it has lost neither its strength nor its nobility.

L. U.

New York City.
January, 1920.

MODERN BRITISH POETRY

Thomas Hardy

Thomas Hardy was born in 1840, and has for years been famous on both sides of the Atlantic as a writer of intense and sombre novels. His *Tess of the D'Urbervilles* and *Jude the Obscure* are possibly his best known, although his *Wessex Tales* and *Life's Little Ironies* are no less imposing.

It was not until he was almost sixty, in 1898 to be precise, that Hardy abandoned prose and challenged attention as a poet. *The Dynasts*, a drama of the Napoleonic Wars, is in three parts, nineteen acts and one hundred and thirty scenes, a massive and most amazing contribution to contemporary art. It is the apotheosis of Hardy the novelist. Lascelles Abercrombie calls this work, which is partly a historical play, partly a visionary drama, "the biggest and most consistent exhibition of fatalism in literature." While its powerful simplicity and tragic impressiveness overshadow his shorter poems, many of his terse lyrics reveal the same vigor and impact of a strong personality. His collected poems were published by The Macmillan Company in 1919 and reveal another phase of one of the greatest living writers of English.

IN TIME OF "THE BREAKING OF NATIONS"

> Only a man harrowing clods
>   In a slow silent walk,
> With an old horse that stumbles and nods
>   Half asleep as they stalk.
>
> Only thin smoke without flame
>   From the heaps of couch grass:
> Yet this will go onward the same
>   Though Dynasties pass.

Yonder a maid and her wight
    Come whispering by;
War's annals will fade into night
    Ere their story die.

GOING AND STAYING

The moving sun-shapes on the spray,
The sparkles where the brook was flowing,
Pink faces, plightings, moonlit May,—
These were the things we wished would stay;
    But they were going.

Seasons of blankness as of snow,
The silent bleed of a world decaying,
The moan of multitudes in woe,—
These were the things we wished would go;
    But they were staying.

THE MAN HE KILLED

(From " The Dynasts")

" Had he and I but met
    By some old ancient inn,
We should have sat us down to wet
    Right many a nipperkin!

" But ranged as infantry,
    And staring face to face,
I shot at him as he at me,
    And killed him in his place.

4

Thomas Hardy

"I shot him dead because—
    Because he was my foe,
Just so: my foe of course he was;
    That's clear enough; although

"He thought he'd 'list, perhaps,
    Off-hand like—just as I—
Was out of work—had sold his traps—
    No other reason why.

"Yes; quaint and curious war is!
    You shoot a fellow down
You'd treat, if met where any bar is,
    Or help to half-a-crown."

Robert Bridges

Robert Bridges was born in 1844 and educated at Eton and Corpus Christi College, Oxford. After traveling extensively, he studied medicine in London and practiced until 1882. Most of his poems, like his occasional plays, are classical in tone as well as treatment. He was appointed poet laureate in 1913, following Alfred Austin. His command of the secrets of rhythm and a subtle versification give his lines a firm delicacy and beauty of pattern.

WINTER NIGHTFALL

The day begins to droop,—
    Its course is done:
But nothing tells the place
    Of the setting sun.

5

Robert Bridges

The hazy darkness deepens,
  And up the lane
You may hear, but cannot see,
  The homing wain.

An engine pants and hums
  In the farm hard by:
Its lowering smoke is lost
  In the lowering sky.

The soaking branches drip,
  And all night through
The dropping will not cease
  In the avenue.

A tall man there in the house
  Must keep his chair:
He knows he will never again
  Breathe the spring air:

His heart is worn with work;
  He is giddy and sick
If he rise to go as far
  As the nearest rick:

He thinks of his morn of life,
  His hale, strong years;
And braves as he may the night
  Of darkness and tears.

Robert Bridges

NIGHTINGALES

Beautiful must be the mountains whence ye come,
And bright in the fruitful valleys the streams, wherefrom
      Ye learn your song:
Where are those starry woods? O might I wander there,
  Among the flowers, which in that heavenly air
      Bloom the year long!

Nay, barren are those mountains and spent the streams:
Our song is the voice of desire, that haunts our dreams,
      A throe of the heart,
Whose pining visions dim, forbidden hopes profound,
  No dying cadence nor long sigh can sound,
      For all our art.

Alone, aloud in the raptured ear of men
We pour our dark nocturnal secret; and then,
      As night is withdrawn
From these sweet-springing meads and bursting boughs of
    May,
  Dream, while the innumerable choir of day
      Welcome the dawn.

Arthur O'Shaughnessy

The Irish-English singer, Arthur William Edgar O'Shaughnessy, was born in London in 1844. He was connected, for a while, with the British Museum, and was transferred later to the Department of Natural History. His first literary success, *Epic of Women* (1870), promised a brilliant future for the young poet, a promise strengthened by his *Music and Moonlight* (1874). Always delicate in health, his hopes were dashed by periods of illness and an early death in London in 1881.

The poem here reprinted is not only O'Shaughnessy's best, but is, because of its perfect blending of music and message, one of the immortal classics of our verse.

ODE

We are the music-makers,
   And we are the dreamers of dreams,
Wandering by lone sea-breakers,
   And sitting by desolate streams;
World-losers and world-forsakers,
   On whom the pale moon gleams:
Yet we are the movers and shakers
   Of the world for ever, it seems.

With wonderful deathless ditties
We build up the world's great cities,
   And out of a fabulous story
   We fashion an empire's glory:
One man with a dream, at pleasure,
   Shall go forth and conquer a crown;
And three with a new song's measure
   Can trample an empire down.

Arthur O'Shaughnessy

We, in the ages lying
    In the buried past of the earth,
Built Nineveh with our sighing,
    And Babel itself with our mirth;
And o'erthrew them with prophesying
    To the old of the new world's worth;
For each age is a dream that is dying,
    Or one that is coming to birth.

William Ernest Henley

William Ernest Henley was born in 1849 and was educated at the Grammar School of Gloucester. From childhood he was afflicted with a tuberculous disease which finally necessitated the amputation of a foot. His *Hospital Verses,* those vivid precursors of current free verse, were a record of the time when he was at the infirmary at Edinburgh; they are sharp with the sights, sensations, even the actual smells of the sick-room. In spite (or, more probably, because) of his continued poor health, Henley never ceased to worship strength and energy; courage and a triumphant belief in a harsh world shine out of the athletic *London Voluntaries* (1892) and the lightest and most musical lyrics in *Hawthorn and Lavender* (1898).

The bulk of Henley's poetry is not great in volume. He has himself explained the small quantity of his work in a Preface to his *Poems,* first published by Charles Scribner's Sons in 1898. " A principal reason," he says, " is that, after spending the better part of my life in the pursuit of poetry, I found myself (about 1877) so utterly unmarketable that I had to own myself beaten in art, and to indict myself to journalism for the next ten years." Later on, he began to write again—" old dusty sheaves were dragged to light; the work of selection and correction was begun; I burned much; I found that, after all, the lyrical instinct had slept—not died."

After a brilliant and varied career (see Preface), devoted mostly to journalism, Henley died in 1903.

INVICTUS

Out of the night that covers me,
   Black as the Pit from pole to pole,
I thank whatever gods may be
   For my unconquerable soul.

In the fell clutch of circumstance
   I have not winced nor cried aloud.
Under the bludgeonings of chance
   My head is bloody, but unbowed.

Beyond this place of wrath and tears
   Looms but the Horror of the shade,
And yet the menace of the years
   Finds, and shall find, me unafraid.

It matters not how strait the gate,
   How charged with punishments the scroll,
I am the master of my fate:
   I am the captain of my soul.

THE BLACKBIRD

The nightingale has a lyre of gold,
   The lark's is a clarion call,
And the blackbird plays but a boxwood flute,
   But I love him best of all.

10

William Ernest Henley

For his song is all of the joy of life,
    And we in the mad, spring weather,
We two have listened till he sang
    Our hearts and lips together.

A BOWL OF ROSES

It was a bowl of roses:
    There in the light they lay,
Languishing, glorying, glowing
    Their life away.

And the soul of them rose like a presence,
    Into me crept and grew,
And filled me with something—some one—
    O, was it you?

BEFORE

Behold me waiting—waiting for the knife.
A little while, and at a leap I storm
The thick sweet mystery of chloroform,
The drunken dark, the little death-in-life.
The gods are good to me: I have no wife,
No innocent child, to think of as I near
The fateful minute; nothing all-too dear
Unmans me for my bout of passive strife.

Yet I am tremulous and a trifle sick,
And, face to face with chance, I shrink a little:
My hopes are strong, my will is something weak.
Here comes the basket? Thank you. I am ready
But, gentlemen my porters, life is brittle:
You carry Cæsar and his fortunes—Steady!

MARGARITÆ SORORI

A late lark twitters from the quiet skies;
And from the west,
Where the sun, his day's work ended,
Lingers as in content,
There falls on the old, grey city
An influence luminous and serene,
A shining peace.

The smoke ascends
In a rosy-and-golden haze. The spires
Shine, and are changed. In the valley
Shadows rise. The lark sings on. The sun,
Closing his benediction,
Sinks, and the darkening air
Thrills with a sense of the triumphing night—
Night with her train of stars
And her great gift of sleep.

So be my passing!
My task accomplished and the long day done,
My wages taken, and in my heart
Some late lark singing,

William Ernest Henley

Let me be gathered to the quiet west,
The sundown splendid and serene,
Death.

Robert Louis Stevenson

Robert Louis Stevenson was born at Edinburgh in 1850. He was at first trained to be a lighthouse engineer, following the profession of his family. However, he studied law instead; was admitted to the bar in 1875; and abandoned law for literature a few years later.

Though primarily a novelist, Stevenson has left one immortal book of poetry which is equally at home in the nursery and the library: *A Child's Garden of Verses* (first published in 1885) is second only to Mother Goose's own collection in its lyrical simplicity and universal appeal. *Underwoods* (1887) and *Ballads* (1890) comprise his entire poetic output. As a genial essayist, he is not unworthy to be ranked with Charles Lamb. As a romancer, his fame rests securely on *Kidnapped*, the unfinished masterpiece, *Weir of Hermiston*, and that eternal classic of youth, *Treasure Island*.

Stevenson died after a long and dogged fight with his illness, in the Samoan Islands in 1894.

SUMMER SUN

Great is the sun, and wide he goes
Through empty heaven without repose;
And in the blue and glowing days
More thick than rain he showers his rays.

Though closer still the blinds we pull
To keep the shady parlour cool,
Yet he will find a chink or two
To slip his golden fingers through.

13

The dusty attic, spider-clad,
He, through the keyhole, maketh glad;
And through the broken edge of tiles
Into the laddered hay-loft smiles.

Meantime his golden face around
He bares to all the garden ground,
And sheds a warm and glittering look
Among the ivy's inmost nook.

Above the hills, along the blue,
Round the bright air with footing true,
To please the child, to paint the rose,
The gardener of the World, he goes.

WINTER-TIME

Late lies the wintry sun a-bed,
A frosty, fiery sleepy-head;
Blinks but an hour or two; and then,
A blood-red orange, sets again.

Before the stars have left the skies,
At morning in the dark I rise;
And shivering in my nakedness,
By the cold candle, bathe and dress.

Close by the jolly fire I sit
To warm my frozen bones a bit;
Or with a reindeer-sled, explore
The colder countries round the door.

When to go out, my nurse doth wrap
Me in my comforter and cap;
The cold wind burns my face, and blows
Its frosty pepper up my nose.

Black are my steps on silver sod;
Thick blows my frosty breath abroad;
And tree and house, and hill and lake,
Are frosted like a wedding-cake.

ROMANCE

I will make you brooches and toys for your delight
Of bird-song at morning and star-shine at night.
I will make a palace fit for you and me,
Of green days in forests and blue days at sea.

I will make my kitchen, and you shall keep your room,
Where white flows the river and bright blows the broom,
And you shall wash your linen and keep your body white
In rainfall at morning and dewfall at night.

And this shall be for music when no one else is near,
The fine song for singing, the rare song to hear!
That only I remember, that only you admire,
Of the broad road that stretches and the roadside fire.

Robert Louis Stevenson

REQUIEM

Under the wide and starry sky
  Dig the grave and let me lie:
Glad did I live and gladly die,
  And I laid me down with a will.

This be the verse you 'grave for me:
  Here he lies where he long'd to be;
Home is the sailor, home from the sea,
  And the hunter home from the hill.

Alice Meynell

Alice Meynell was born in London in 1850. She was educated at home and spent a great part of her childhood in Italy. She has written little, but that little is on an extremely high plane; her verses are simple, pensive and always distinguished. The best of her work is in *Poems* (1903).

A THRUSH BEFORE DAWN

A voice peals in this end of night
  A phrase of notes resembling stars,
Single and spiritual notes of light.
  What call they at my window-bars?
    The South, the past, the day to be,
    An ancient infelicity.

16

Alice Meynell

Darkling, deliberate, what sings
  This wonderful one, alone, at peace?
What wilder things than song, what things
  Sweeter than youth, clearer than Greece,
    Dearer than Italy, untold
    Delight, and freshness centuries old?

And first first-loves, a multitude,
  The exaltation of their pain;
Ancestral childhood long renewed;
  And midnights of invisible rain;
    And gardens, gardens, night and day,
    Gardens and childhood all the way.

What Middle Ages passionate,
  O passionless voice! What distant bells
Lodged in the hills, what palace state
  Illyrian! For it speaks, it tells,
    Without desire, without dismay,
    Some morrow and some yesterday.

All-natural things! But more—Whence came
  This yet remoter mystery?
How do these starry notes proclaim
  A graver still divinity?
    This hope, this sanctity of fear?
    O innocent throat! O human ear!

Fiona Macleod

(*William Sharp*)

William Sharp was born at Garthland Place, Scotland, in 1855. He wrote several volumes of biography and criticism, published a book of plays greatly influenced by Maeterlinck (*Vistas*) and was editor of "The Canterbury Poets" series.

His feminine *alter ego*, Fiona Macleod, was a far different personality. Sharp actually believed himself possessed of another spirit; under the spell of this other self, he wrote several volumes of Celtic tales, beautiful tragic romances and no little unusual poetry. Of the prose stories written by Fiona Macleod, the most barbaric and vivid are those collected in *The Sin-Eater and Other Tales;* the longer *Pharais, A Romance of the Isles,* is scarcely less unique.

In the ten years, 1882-1891, William Sharp published four volumes of rather undistinguished verse. In 1896 *From the Hills of Dream* appeared over the signature of Fiona Macleod; *The Hour of Beauty,* an even more distinctive collection, followed shortly. Both poetry and prose were always the result of two sharply differentiated moods constantly fluctuating; the emotional mood was that of Fiona Macleod, the intellectual and, it must be admitted the more arresting, was that of William Sharp.

He died in 1905.

THE VALLEY OF SILENCE

In the secret Valley of Silence
    No breath doth fall;
No wind stirs in the branches;
    No bird doth call:
As on a white wall
    A breathless lizard is still,
So silence lies on the valley
    Breathlessly still.

Fiona Macleod

In the dusk-grown heart of the valley
      An altar rises white:
No rapt priest bends in awe
            Before its silent light:
            But sometimes a flight
                  Of breathless words of prayer
            White-wing'd enclose the altar,
                  Eddies of prayer.

THE VISION

In a fair place
      Of whin and grass,
      I heard feet pass
      Where no one was.

I saw a face
      Bloom like a flower—
      Nay, as the rainbow-shower
      Of a tempestuous hour.

It was not man, or woman:
It was not human:
      But, beautiful and wild,
      Terribly undefiled,
      I knew an unborn child.

Oscar Wilde

Oscar Wilde was born at Dublin, Ireland, in 1856, and even
as an undergraduate at Oxford he was marked for a brilliant
career. When he was a trifle over 21 years of age, he won the
Newdigate Prize with his poem *Ravenna*.

19

Oscar Wilde

Giving himself almost entirely to prose, he speedily became known as a writer of brilliant epigrammatic essays and even more brilliant paradoxical plays such as *An Ideal Husband* and *The Importance of Being Earnest.* His aphorisms and flippancies were quoted everywhere; his fame as a wit was only surpassed by his notoriety as an æsthete. (See Preface.)

Most of his poems in prose (such as *The Happy Prince, The Birthday of the Infanta* and *The Fisherman and His Soul*) are more imaginative and richly colored than his verse; but in one long poem, *The Ballad of Reading Gaol* (1898), he sounded his deepest, simplest and most enduring note. Prison was, in many ways, a regeneration for Wilde. It not only produced *The Ballad of Reading Gaol* but made possible his most poignant piece of writing, *De Profundis,* only a small part of which has been published. *Salomé,* which has made the author's name a household word, was originally written in French in 1892 and later translated into English by Lord Alfred Douglas, accompanied by the famous illustrations by Aubrey Beardsley. More recently this heated drama, based on the story of Herod and Herodias, was made into an opera by Richard Strauss.

Wilde's society plays, flashing and cynical, were the forerunners of Bernard Shaw's audacious and far more searching ironies. One sees the origin of a whole school of drama in such epigrams as "The history of woman is the history of the worst form of tyranny the world has ever known: the tyranny of the weak over the strong. It is the only tyranny that lasts." Or "There is only one thing in the world worse than being talked about, and that is not being talked about."

Wilde died at Paris, November 30, 1900.

REQUIESCAT

Tread lightly, she is near
Under the snow,
Speak gently, she can hear
The daisies grow.

All her bright golden hair
    Tarnished with rust,
She that was young and fair
    Fallen to dust.

Lily-like, white as snow,
    She hardly knew
She was a woman, so
    Sweetly she grew.

Coffin-board, heavy stone,
    Lie on her breast;
I vex my heart alone,
    She is at rest.

Peace, peace; she cannot hear
    Lyre or sonnet;
All my life's buried here,
    Heap earth upon it.

IMPRESSION DU MATIN

The Thames nocturne of blue and gold
    Changed to a harmony in grey;
    A barge with ochre-coloured hay
Dropt from the wharf: and chill and cold

The yellow fog came creeping down
    The bridges, till the houses' walls
    Seemed changed to shadows, and St. Paul's
Loomed like a bubble o'er the town.

Oscar Wilde

Then suddenly arose the clang
  Of waking life; the streets were stirred
  With country waggons; and a bird
Flew to the glistening roofs and sang.

But one pale woman all alone,
  The daylight kissing her wan hair,
  Loitered beneath the gas lamps' flare,
With lips of flame and heart of stone.

John Davidson

John Davidson was born at Barrhead, Renfrewshire, in 1857.
His *Ballads and Songs* (1895) and *New Ballads* (1897) at-
tained a sudden but too short-lived popularity, and his great
promise was quenched by an apathetic public and by his own
growing disillusion and despair. His sombre yet direct poetry
never tired of repeating his favorite theme: "Man is but the
Universe grown conscious."
Davidson died by his own hand in 1909.

A BALLAD OF HELL

' A letter from my love to-day!
  Oh, unexpected, dear appeal!'
She struck a happy tear away,
  And broke the crimson seal.

' My love, there is no help on earth,
  No help in heaven; the dead-man's bell
Must toll our wedding; our first hearth
  Must be the well-paved floor of hell.'

22

John Davidson

The colour died from out her face,
  Her eyes like ghostly candles shone;
She cast dread looks about the place,
  Then clenched her teeth and read right on.

'I may not pass the prison door;
  Here must I rot from day to day,
Unless I wed whom I abhor,
  My cousin, Blanche of Valencay.

'At midnight with my dagger keen,
  I'll take my life; it must be so.
Meet me in hell to-night, my queen,
  For weal and woe.'

She laughed although her face was wan,
  She girded on her golden belt,
She took her jewelled ivory fan,
  And at her glowing missal knelt.

Then rose, 'And am I mad?' she said:
  She broke her fan, her belt untied;
With leather girt herself instead,
  And stuck a dagger at her side.

She waited, shuddering in her room,
  Till sleep had fallen on all the house.
She never flinched; she faced her doom:
  They two must sin to keep their vows.

John Davidson

Then out into the night she went,
　And, stooping, crept by hedge and tree;
Her rose-bush flung a snare of scent,
　And caught a happy memory.

She fell, and lay a minute's space;
　She tore the sward in her distress;
The dewy grass refreshed her face;
　She rose and ran with lifted dress.

She started like a morn-caught ghost
　Once when the moon came out and stood
To watch; the naked road she crossed,
　And dived into the murmuring wood.

The branches snatched her streaming cloak;
　A live thing shrieked; she made no stay!
She hurried tc the trysting-oak—
　Right well she knew the way.

Without a pause she bared her breast,
　And drove her dagger home and fell,
And lay like one that takes her rest,
　And died and wakened up in hell.

She bathed her spirit in the flame,
　And near the centre took her post;
From all sides to her ears there came
　The dreary anguish of the lost.

John Davidson

The devil started at hei side,
    Comely, and tall, and black as jet.
' I am young Malespina's bride;
    Has he come hither yet? '

' My poppet, welcome to your bed.'
    ' Is Malespina here? '
' Not he! To-morrow he must wed
    His cousin Blanche, my dear! '

' You lie, he died with me to-night.'
    ' Not he! it was a plot ' . . . ' You lie.'
' My dear, I never lie outright.'
    ' We died at midnight, he and I.'

The devil went. Without a groan
    She, gathered up in one fierce prayer,
Took root in hell's midst all alone,
    And waited for him there.

She dared to make herself at home
    Amidst the wail, the uneasy stir.
The blood-stained flame that filled the dome,
    Scentless and silent, shrouded her.

How long she stayed I cannot tell;
    But when she felt his perfidy,
She marched across the floor of hell;
    And all the damned stood up to see.

John Davidson

The devil stopped her at the brink:
    She shook him off; she cried, 'Away!'
'My dear, you have gone mad, I think.'
    'I was betrayed: I will not stay.'

Across the weltering deep she ran;
    A stranger thing was never seen:
The damned stood silent to a man;
    They saw the great gulf set between.

To her it seemed a meadow fair;
    And flowers sprang up about her feet
She entered heaven; she climbed the stair
    And knelt down at the mercy-seat.

Seraphs and saints with one great voice
    Welcomed that soul that knew not fear.
Amazed to find it could rejoice,
    Hell raised a hoarse, half-human cheer.

IMAGINATION

(*From " New Year's Eve "*)

There is a dish to hold the sea,
    A brazier to contain the sun,
A compass for the galaxy,
    A voice to wake the dead and done!

John Davidson

That minister of ministers,
    Imagination, gathers up
The undiscovered Universe,
    Like jewels in a jasper cup.

Its flame can mingle north and south;
    Its accent with the thunder strive;
The ruddy sentence of its mouth
    Can make the ancient dead alive.

The mart of power, the fount of will,
    The form and mould of every star,
The source and bound of good and ill,
    The key of all the things that are,

Imagination, new and strange
    In every age, can turn the year;
Can shift the poles and lightly change
    The mood of men, the world's career.

William Watson

William Watson was born at Burley-in-Wharfedale, York-shire, August 2, 1858. He achieved his first wide success through his long and eloquent poems on Wordsworth, Shelley, and Tennyson—poems that attempted, and sometimes success-fully, to combine the manners of these masters. *The Hope of the World* (1897) contains some of his most characteristic verse.

It was understood that he would be appointed poet laureate upon the death of Alfred Austin. But some of his radical and semi-political poems are supposed to have displeased the pow-

27

ers at Court, and the honor went to Robert Bridges. His best work, which is notable for its dignity and moulded imagination, may be found in *Selected Poems,* published in 1903 by John Lane Co.

ODE IN MAY [1]

Let me go forth, and share
The overflowing Sun
With one wise friend, or one
Better than wise, being fair,
Where the pewit wheels and dips
On heights of bracken and ling,
And Earth, unto her leaflet tips,
Tingles with the Spring.

What is so sweet and dear
As a prosperous morn in May,
The confident prime of the day,
And the dauntless youth of the year,
When nothing that asks for bliss,
Asking aright, is denied,
And half of the world a bridegroom is,
And half of the world a bride?

The Song of Mingling flows,
Grave, ceremonial, pure,
As once, from lips that endure,
The cosmic descant rose,

[1] From *The Hope of the World* by William Watson. Copyright, 1897, by John Lane Company. Reprinted by permission of the publishers.

William Watson

When the temporal lord of life,
Going his golden way,
Had taken a wondrous maid to wife
That long had said him nay.

For of old the Sun, our sire,
Came wooing the mother of men,
Earth, that was virginal then,
Vestal fire to his fire.
Silent her bosom and coy,
But the strong god sued and pressed;
And born of their starry nuptial joy
Are all that drink of her breast.

And the triumph of him that begot,
And the travail of her that bore,
Behold, they are evermore
As warp and weft in our lot.
We are children of splendour and flame,
Of shuddering, also, and tears.
Magnificent out of the dust we came,
And abject from the Spheres.

O bright irresistible lord,
We are fruit of Earth's womb, each one,
And fruit of thy loins, O Sun,
Whence first was the seed outpoured.
To thee as our Father we bow,
Forbidden thy Father to see,
Who is older and greater than thou, as
    thou
Art greater and older than we.

Thou art but as a word of his speech,
Thou art but as a wave of his hand;
Thou art brief as a glitter of sand
'Twixt tide and tide on his beach;
Thou art less than a spark of his fire,
Or a moment's mood of his soul:
Thou art lost in the notes on the lips of
    his choir
That chant the chant of the Whole.

ESTRANGEMENT [1]

So, without overt breach, we fall apart,
Tacitly sunder—neither you nor I
Conscious of one intelligible Why,
And both, from severance, winning equal smart.
So, with resigned and acquiescent heart,
Whene'er your name on some chance lip may lie,
I seem to see an alien shade pass by,
A spirit wherein I have no lot or part.

Thus may a captive, in some fortress grim,
From casual speech betwixt his warders, learn
That June on her triumphal progress goes
Through arched and bannered woodlands; while
        for him
She is a legend emptied of concern,
And idle is the rumour of the rose.

[1] From *The Hope of the World* by William Watson. Copyright, 1897, by John Lane Company. Reprinted by permission of the publishers.

William Watson

SONG

April, April,
Laugh thy girlish laughter;
Then, the moment after,
Weep thy girlish tears,
April, that mine ears
Like a lover greetest,
If I tell thee, sweetest,
All my hopes and fears.
April, April,
Laugh thy golden laughter,
But, the moment after,
Weep thy golden tears!

Francis Thompson

Born in 1859 at Preston, Francis Thompson was educated at
Owen's College, Manchester. Later he tried all manner of
strange ways of earning a living. He was, at various times,
assistant in a boot-shop, medical student, collector for a book
seller and homeless vagabond; there was a period in his life
when he sold matches on the streets of London. He was
discovered in terrible poverty (having given up everything ex-
cept poetry and opium) by the editor of a magazine to which
he had sent some verses the year before. Almost immediately
thereafter he became famous. His exalted mysticism is seen
at its purest in " A Fallen Yew " and " The Hound of Heaven."
Coventry Patmore, the distinguished poet of an earlier period,
says of the latter poem, which is unfortunately too long to

quote, "It is one of the very few *great* odes of which our language can boast."

Thompson died, after a fragile and spasmodic life, in St. John's Wood in November, 1907.

DAISY

Where the thistle lifts a purple crown
  Six foot out of the turf,
And the harebell shakes on the windy hill—
  O breath of the distant surf!—

The hills look over on the South,
  And southward dreams the sea;
And with the sea-breeze hand in hand
  Came innocence and she.

Where 'mid the gorse the raspberry
  Red for the gatherer springs;
Two children did we stray and talk
  Wise, idle, childish things.

She listened with big-lipped surprise,
  Breast-deep 'mid flower and spine:
Her skin was like a grape whose veins
  Run snow instead of wine.

She knew not those sweet words she spake,
  Nor knew her own sweet way;
But there's never a bird, so sweet a song
  Thronged in whose throat all day.

Francis Thompson

Oh, there were flowers in Storrington
    On the turf and on the spray;
But the sweetest flower on Sussex hills
    Was the Daisy-flower that day!

Her beauty smoothed earth's furrowed face.
    She gave me tokens three:—
A look, a word of her winsome mouth,
    And a wild raspberry.

A berry red, a guileless look,
    A still word,—strings of sand!
And yet they made my wild, wild heart
    Fly down to her little hand.

For standing artless as the air,
    And candid as the skies,
She took the berries with her hand,
    And the love with her sweet eyes.

The fairest things have fleetest end,
    Their scent survives their close:
But the rose's scent is bitterness
    To him that loved the rose.

She looked a little wistfully,
    Then went her sunshine way:—
The sea's eye had a mist on it,
    And the leaves fell from the day.

She went her unremembering way,
 She went and left in me
The pang of all the partings gone,
 And partings yet to be.

She left me marvelling why my soul
 Was sad that she was glad;
At all the sadness in the sweet,
 The sweetness in the sad.

Still, still I seemed to see her, still
 Look up with soft replies,
And take the berries with her hand,
 And the love with her lovely eyes.

Nothing begins, and nothing ends,
 That is not paid with moan,
For we are born in other's pain,
 And perish in our own.

TO OLIVIA

I fear to love thee, Sweet, because
Love's the ambassador of loss;
White flake of childhood, clinging so
To my soiled raiment, thy shy snow
At tenderest touch will shrink and go.
Love me not, delightful child.
My heart, by many snares beguiled,
Has grown timorous and wild.

It would fear thee not at all,
Wert thou not so harmless-small.
Because thy arrows, not yet dire,
Are still unbarbed with destined fire,
I fear thee more than hadst thou stood
Full-panoplied in womanhood.

AN ARAB LOVE-SONG

The hunchèd camels of the night [1]
Trouble the bright
And silver waters of the moon.
The Maiden of the Morn will soon
Through Heaven stray and sing,
Star gathering.

Now while the dark about our loves is strewn,
Light of my dark, blood of my heart, O come!
And night will catch her breath up, and be dumb.

Leave thy father, leave thy mother
And thy brother;
Leave the black tents of thy tribe apart!
Am I not thy father and thy brother,
And thy mother?
And thou—what needest with thy tribe's black
        tents
Who hast the red pavilion of my heart?

[1] (Cloud-shapes observed by travellers in the East.)

A. E. Housman

A. E. Housman was born March 26, 1859, and, after a classical education, he was, for ten years, a Higher Division Clerk in H. M. Patent Office. Later in life, he became a teacher.

Housman has published only one volume of original verse, but that volume (*A Shropshire Lad*) is known wherever modern English poetry is read. Originally published in 1896, when Housman was almost 37, it is evident that many of these lyrics were written when the poet was much younger. Echoing the frank pessimism of Hardy and the harder cynicism of Heine, Housman struck a lighter and more buoyant note. Underneath his dark ironies, there is a rustic humor that has many subtle variations. From a melodic standpoint, *A Shropshire Lad* is a collection of exquisite, haunting and almost perfect songs.

Housman has been a professor of Latin since 1892 and, besides his immortal set of lyrics, has edited Juvenal and the books of Manlius.

REVEILLÉ

Wake: the silver dusk returning
   Up the beach of darkness brims,
And the ship of sunrise burning
   Strands upon the eastern rims.

Wake: the vaulted shadow shatters,
   Trampled to the floor it spanned,
And the tent of night in tatters
   Straws the sky-pavilioned land.

Up, lad, up, 'tis late for lying:
   Hear the drums of morning play;
Hark, the empty highways crying
   " Who'll beyond the hills away?"

A. E. Housman

Towns and countries woo together,
  Forelands beacon, belfries call;
Never lad that trod on leather
  Lived to feast his heart with all.

Up, lad: thews that lie and cumber
  Sunlit pallets never thrive;
Morns abed and daylight slumber
  Were not meant for man alive.

Clay lies still, but blood's a rover;
  Breath's a ware that will not keep.
Up, lad: when the journey's over
  There'll be time enough to sleep.

WHEN I WAS ONE-AND-TWENTY

When I was one-and-twenty
  I heard a wise man say,
" Give crowns and pounds and guineas
  But not your heart away;
Give pearls away and rubies
  But keep your fancy free."
But I was one-and-twenty,
  No use to talk to me.

When I was one-and-twenty
  I heard him say again,
" The heart out of the bosom
  Was never given in vain;

37

'Tis paid with sighs a-plenty
    And sold for endless rue."
And I am two-and-twenty,
    And oh, 'tis true, 'tis true.

WITH RUE MY HEART IS LADEN

With rue my heart is laden
    For golden friends I had,
For many a rose-lipt maiden
    And many a lightfoot lad.

By brooks too broad for leaping
    The lightfoot boys are laid;
The rose-lipt girls are sleeping
    In fields where roses fade.

TO AN ATHLETE DYING YOUNG

The time you won your town the race
We chaired you through the market-place;
Man and boy stood cheering by,
And home we brought you shoulder-high.

To-day, the road all runners come,
Shoulder-high we bring you home,
And set you at your threshold down,
Townsman of a stiller town.

A. E. Housman

Smart lad, to slip betimes away
From fields where glory does not stay,
And early though the laurel grows
It withers quicker than the rose.

Eyes the shady night has shut
Cannot see the record cut,
And silence sounds no worse than cheers
After earth has stopped the ears:

Now you will not swell the rout
Of lads that wore their honours out,
Runners whom renown outran
And the name died before the man.

So set, before its echoes fade,
The fleet foot on the sill of shade,
And hold to the low lintel up
The still-defended challenge-cup.

And round that early-laurelled head
Will flock to gaze the strengthless dead,
And find unwithered on its curls
The garland briefer than a girl's.

"LOVELIEST OF TREES"

Loveliest of trees, the cherry now
Is hung with bloom along the bough,
And stands about the woodland ride
Wearing white for Eastertide.

A. E. Housman

Now, of my threescore years and ten,
Twenty will not come again,
And take from seventy springs a score,
It only leaves me fifty more.

And since to look at things in bloom
Fifty springs are little room,
About the woodlands I will go
To see the cherry hung with snow.

Douglas Hyde

Doctor Douglas Hyde was born in Roscommon County, Ireland in, as nearly as can be ascertained, 1860. One of the most brilliant Irish scholars of his day, he has worked indefatigably for the cause of his native letters. He has written a comprehensive history of Irish literature; has compiled, edited and translated into English the *Love Songs of Connaught;* is President of The Irish National Literary Society; and is the author of innumerable poems in Gaelic—far more than he ever wrote in English. His collections of Irish folk-lore and poetry were among the most notable contributions to the Celtic revival; they were (see Preface), to a large extent, responsible for it. Since 1909 he has been Professor of Modern Irish in University Collge, Dublin.

The poem which is here quoted is one of his many brilliant and reanimating translations. In its music and its peculiar rhyme-scheme, it reproduces the peculiar flavor as well as the meter of the West Irish original.

I SHALL NOT DIE FOR THEE

For thee, I shall not die,
  Woman of high fame and name;
Foolish men thou mayest slay
  I and they are not the same.

Douglas Hyde

Why should I expire
   For the fire of an eye,
Slender waist or swan-like limb,
   Is't for them that I should die?

The round breasts, the fresh skin,
   Cheeks crimson, hair so long and rich;
Indeed, indeed, I shall not die,
   Please God, not I, for any such.

The golden hair, the forehead thin,
   The chaste mien, the gracious ease,
The rounded heel, the languid tone,—
   Fools alone find death from these.

Thy sharp wit, thy perfect calm,
   Thy thin palm like foam o' the sea;
Thy white neck, thy blue eye,
   I shall not die for thee.

Woman, graceful as the swan,
   A wise man did nurture me.
Little palm, white neck, bright eye,
   I shall not die for ye.

Amy Levy

Amy Levy, a singularly gifted Jewess, was born at Clapham, in 1861. A fiery young poet, she burdened her own intensity with the sorrows of her race. She wrote one novel, *Reuben*

41

Sachs, and two volumes of poetry—the more distinctive of the two being half-pathetically and half-ironically entitled *A Minor Poet* (1884). After several years of brooding introspection, she committed suicide in 1889 at the age of 28.

EPITAPH

(*On a commonplace person who died in bed*)

This is the end of him, here he lies:
The dust in his throat, the worm in his eyes,
The mould in his mouth, the turf on his breast;
This is the end of him, this is best.
He will never lie on his couch awake,
Wide-eyed, tearless, till dim daybreak.
Never again will he smile and smile
When his heart is breaking all the while.
He will never stretch out his hands in vain
Groping and groping—never again.
Never ask for bread, get a stone instead,
Never pretend that the stone is bread;
Nor sway and sway 'twixt the false and true,
Weighing and noting the long hours through.
Never ache and ache with the choked-up sighs;
This is the end of him, here he lies.

IN THE MILE END ROAD

How like her! But 'tis she herself,
    Comes up the crowded street,
How little did I think, the morn,
    My only love to meet!

Amy Levy

Who else that motion and that mien?
   Whose else that airy tread?
For one strange moment I forgot
   My only love was dead.

Katharine Tynan Hinkson

Katharine Tynan was born at Dublin in 1861, and educated
at the Convent of St. Catherine at Drogheda. She married
Henry Hinkson, a lawyer and author, in 1893. Her poetry is
largely actuated by religious themes, and much of her verse is
devotional and yet distinctive. In *New Poems* (1911) she is
at her best; graceful, meditative and with occasional notes of
deep pathos.

SHEEP AND LAMBS

All in the April morning,
   April airs were abroad;
The sheep with their little lambs
   Pass'd me by on the road.

The sheep with their little lambs
   Pass'd me by on the road;
All in an April evening
   I thought on the Lamb of God.

The lambs were weary, and crying
   With a weak human cry;
I thought on the Lamb of God
   Going meekly to die.

43

Katharine Tynan Hinkson

Up in the blue, blue mountains
    Dewy pastures are sweet:
Rest for the little bodies,
    Rest for the little feet.

Rest for the Lamb of God
    Up on the hill-top green;
Only a cross of shame
    Two stark crosses between.

All in the April evening,
    April airs were abroad;
I saw the sheep with their lambs,
    And thought on the Lamb of God.

ALL-SOULS

The door of Heaven is on the latch
    To-night, and many a one is fain
To go home for one's night's watch
    With his love again.

Oh, where the father and mother sit
    There's a drift of dead leaves at the door
Like pitter-patter of little feet
    That come no more.

Their thoughts are in the night and cold,
    Their tears are heavier than the clay,
But who is this at the threshold
    So young and gay?

Katharine Tynan Hinkson

They are come from the land o' the young,
   They have forgotten how to weep;
Words of comfort on the tongue,
   And a kiss to keep.

They sit down and they stay awhile,
   Kisses and comfort none shall lack;
At morn they steal forth with a smile
   And a long look back.

Owen Seaman

One of the most delightful of English versifiers, Owen Seaman, was born in 1861. After receiving a classical education, he became Professor of Literature and began to write for Punch in 1894. In 1906 he was made editor of that internationally famous weekly, remaining in that capacity ever since. He was knighted in 1914. As a writer of light verse and as a parodist, his agile work has delighted a generation of admirers. Some of his most adroit lines may be found in his *In Cap and Bells* (1902) and *The Battle of the Bays* (1892).

TO AN OLD FOGEY

(Who Contends that Christmas is Played Out)

O frankly bald and obviously stout!
   And so you find that Christmas as a fête
Dispassionately viewed, is getting out
      Of date.

Owen Seaman

The studied festal air is overdone;
  The humour of it grows a little thin;
You fail, in fact, to gather where the fun
    Comes in.

Visions of very heavy meals arise
  That tend to make your organism shiver;
Roast beef that irks, and pies that agonise
    The liver;

Those pies at which you annually wince,
  Hearing the tale how happy months will follow
Proportioned to the total mass of mince
    You swallow.

Visions of youth whose reverence is scant,
  Who with the brutal *verve* of boyhood's prime
Insist on being taken to the pant-
    -omime.

Of infants, sitting up extremely late,
  Who run you on toboggans down the stair;
Or make you fetch a rug and simulate
    A bear.

This takes your faultless trousers at the knees,
  The other hurts them rather more behind;
And both effect a fracture in your ease
    Of mind.

46

My good dyspeptic, this will never do;
  Your weary withers must be sadly wrung!
Yet once I well believe that even you
    Were young.

Time was when you devoured, like other boys,
  Plum-pudding sequent on a turkey-hen;
With cracker-mottos hinting of the joys
    Of men.

Time was when 'mid the maidens you would pull
  The fiery raisin with profound delight;
When sprigs of mistletoe seemed beautiful
    And right.

Old Christmas changes not! Long, long ago
  He won the treasure of eternal youth;
Yours is the dotage—if you want to know
    The truth.

Come, now, I'll cure your case, and ask no fee:—
  Make others' happiness this once your own;
All else may pass: that joy can never be
    Outgrown!

THOMAS OF THE LIGHT HEART

Facing the guns, he jokes as well
  As any Judge upon the Bench;
Between the crash of shell and shell
  His laughter rings along the trench;

Owen Seaman

He seems immensely tickled by a
Projectile while he calls a " Black Maria."

He whistles down the day-long road,
   And, when the chilly shadows fall
And heavier hangs the weary load,
   Is he down-hearted? Not at all.
'Tis then he takes a light and airy
View of the tedious route to Tipperary.[1]

His songs are not exactly hymns;
   He never learned them in the choir;
And yet they brace his dragging limbs
   Although they miss the sacred fire;
Although his choice and cherished gems
Do not include " The Watch upon the
     Thames."

He takes to fighting as a game;
   He does no talking, through his hat,
Of holy missions; all the same
   He has his faith—be sure of that;
He'll not disgrace his sporting breed,
Nor play what isn't cricket. There's his
     creed.

[1] "*It's a long way to Tipperary,*" the most popular song of
the Allied armies during the World's War.

Henry Newbolt

Henry Newbolt was born at Bilston in 1862. His early work was frankly imitative of Tennyson; he even attempted to add to the Arthurian legends with a drama in blank verse entitled *Mordred* (1895). It was not until he wrote his sea-ballads that he struck his own note. With the publication of *Admirals All* (1897) his fame was widespread. The popularity of his lines was due not so much to the subject-matter of Newbolt's verse as to the breeziness of his music, the solid beat of rhythm, the vigorous swing of his stanzas.

In 1898 Newbolt published *The Island Race,* which contains about thirty more of his buoyant songs of the sea. Besides being a poet, Newbolt has written many essays and his critical volume, *A New Study of English Poetry* (1917), is a collection of articles that are both analytical and alive.

DRAKE'S DRUM

Drake he's in his hammock an' a thousand mile away,
 (Capten, art tha sleepin' there below?)
Slung atween the round shot in Nombre Dios Bay,
 An' dreamin' arl the time o' Plymouth Hoe.
Yarnder lumes the island, yarnder lie the ships,
 Wi' sailor lads a-dancin' heel-an'-toe,
An' the shore-lights flashin', an' the night-tide dashin',
 He sees et arl so plainly as he saw et long ago.

Drake he was a Devon man, an' ruled the Devon seas,
 (Capten, art tha sleepin' there below?),
Rovin' tho' his death fell, he went wi' heart at ease,
 An' dreamin' arl the time o' Plymouth Hoe,
" Take my drum to England, hang et by the shore,
 Strike et when your powder's runnin' low;
If the Dons sight Devon, I'll quit the port o' Heaven,
 An' drum them up the Channel as we drummed
  them long ago."

Henry Newbolt

Drake he's in his hammock till the great Armadas come,
    (Capten, art tha sleepin' there below?),
Slung atween the round shot, listenin' for the drum,
    An' dreamin' arl the time o' Plymouth Hoe.
Call him on the deep sea, call him up the Sound,
    Call him when ye sail to meet the foe;
Where the old trade's plyin' an' the old flag flyin',
    They shall find him, ware an' wakin', as they found
        him long ago.

Arthur Symons

Born in 1865, Arthur Symons' first few publications revealed an intellectual rather than an emotional passion. Those volumes were full of the artifice of the period, but Symons's technical skill and frequent analysis often saved the poems from complete decadence. His later books are less imitative; the influence of Verlaine and Baudelaire is not so apparent; the sophistication is less cynical, the sensuousness more restrained. His various collections of essays and stories reflect the same peculiar blend of rich intellectuality and perfumed romanticism that one finds in his most characteristic poems.

Of his many volumes in prose, *Spiritual Adventures* (1905), while obviously influenced by Walter Pater, is by far the most original; a truly unique volume of psychological short stories. The best of his poetry up to 1902 was collected in two volumes, *Poems,* published by John Lane Co. *The Fool of the World* appeared in 1907.

IN THE WOOD OF FINVARA

I have grown tired of sorrow and human tears;
Life is a dream in the night, a fear among fears,
A naked runner lost in a storm of spears.

50

I have grown tired of rapture and love's desire;
Love is a flaming heart, and its flames aspire
Till they cloud the soul in the smoke of a windy
    fire.

I would wash the dust of the world in a soft green
    flood;
Here between sea and sea, in the fairy wood,
I have found a delicate, wave-green solitude.

Here, in the fairy wood, between sea and sea,
I have heard the song of a fairy bird in a tree,
And the peace that is not in the world has flown
    to me.

MODERN BEAUTY

I am the torch, she saith, and what to me
If the moth die of me? I am the flame
Of Beauty, and I burn that all may see
Beauty, and I have neither joy nor shame,
But live with that clear light of perfect fire
Which is to men the death of their desire.

I am Yseult and Helen, I have seen
Troy burn, and the most loving knight lie dead.
The world has been my mirror, time has been
My breath upon the glass; and men have said,
Age after age, in rapture and despair,
Love's poor few words, before my image there.

Arthur Symons

I live, and am immortal; in my eyes
The sorrow of the world, and on my lips
The joy of life, mingle to make me wise;
Yet now the day is darkened with eclipse:
Who is there still lives for beauty? Still am I
The torch, but where's the moth that still dares die?

William Butler Yeats

Born at Sandymount, Dublin, in 1865, the son of John B. Yeats, the Irish artist, the greater part of William Butler Yeats' childhood was spent in Sligo. Here he became imbued with the power and richness of native folk-lore; he drank in the racy quality through the quaint fairy stories and old wives' tales of the Irish peasantry. (Later he published a collection of these same stories.)

It was in the activities of a "Young Ireland" society that Yeats became identified with the new spirit; he dreamed of a national poetry that would be written in English and yet would be definitely Irish. In a few years he became one of the leaders in the Celtic revival. He worked incessantly for the cause, both as propagandist and playwright; and, though his mysticism at times seemed the product of a cult rather than a Celt, his symbolic dramas were acknowledged to be full of a haunting, other-world spirituality. (See Preface.) *The Hour Glass* (1904), his second volume of "Plays for an Irish Theatre," includes his best one-act dramas with the exception of his unforgettable *The Land of Heart's Desire* (1894). *The Wind Among the Reeds* (1899) contains several of his most beautiful and characteristic poems.

Others who followed Yeats have intensified the Irish drama; they have established a closer contact between the peasant and poet. No one, however, has had so great a part in the shaping of modern drama in Ireland as Yeats. His *Deirdre* (1907), a beautiful retelling of the great Gaelic legend, is far more dramatic than the earlier plays; it is particularly interesting to

read with Synge's more idiomatic play on the same theme,
Deirdre of the Sorrows.

The poems of Yeats which are quoted here reveal him in
his most lyric and musical vein.

THE LAKE ISLE OF INNISFREE

I will arise and go now, and go to Innisfree,
And a small cabin build there, of clay and wattles made;
Nine bean rows will I have there, a hive for the honey bee,
    And live alone in the bee-loud glade.

And I shall have some peace there, for peace comes
                dropping slow,
Dropping from the veils of the morning to where the
                cricket sings;
There midnight's all a glimmer, and noon a purple glow,
    And evening full of the linnet's wings.

I will arise and go now, for always night and day
I hear lake water lapping with low sounds by the shore;
While I stand on the roadway, or on the pavements gray,
    I hear it in the deep heart's core.

THE SONG OF THE OLD MOTHER

I rise in the dawn, and I kneel and blow
Till the seed of the fire flicker and glow.
And then I must scrub, and bake, and sweep,
Till stars are beginning to blink and peep;

53

But the young lie long and dream in their bed
Of the matching of ribbons, the blue and the red,
And their day goes over in idleness,
And they sigh if the wind but lift up a tress.
While I must work, because I am old
And the seed of the fire gets feeble and cold.

THE CAP AND BELLS

A Queen was beloved by a jester,
　And once when the owls grew still
He made his soul go upward
　And stand on her window sill.

In a long and straight blue garment,
　It talked before morn was white,
And it had grown wise by thinking
　Of a footfall hushed and light.

But the young queen would not listen;
　She rose in her pale nightgown,
She drew in the brightening casement
　And pushed the brass bolt down.

He bade his heart go to her,
　When the bats cried out no more,
In a red and quivering garment
　It sang to her through the door.

The tongue of it sweet with dreaming
   Of a flutter of flower-like hair,
But she took up her fan from the table
   And waved it off on the air.

'I've cap and bells,' he pondered,
   'I will send them to her and die.'
And as soon as the morn had whitened
   He left them where she went by.

She laid them upon her bosom,
   Under a cloud of her hair,
And her red lips sang them a love song.
   The stars grew out of the air.

She opened her door and her window,
   And the heart and the soul came through,
To her right hand came the red one,
   To her left hand came the blue.

They set up a noise like crickets,
   A chattering wise and sweet,
And her hair was a folded flower,
   And the quiet of love her feet.

AN OLD SONG RESUNG

Down by the salley gardens my love and I did meet;
She passed the salley gardens with little snow-white feet.
She bid me take love easy, as the leaves grow on the tree;
But I, being young and foolish, with her would not agree.

William Butler Yeats

In a field by the river my love and I did stand,
And on my leaning shoulder she laid her snow-white hand.
She bid me take life easy, as the grass grows on the weirs;
But I was young and foolish, and now am full of tears.

Rudyard Kipling

Born at Bombay, India, December 30, 1865, Rudyard Kipling, the author of a dozen contemporary classics, was educated in England. He returned, however, to India and took a position on the staff of "The Lahore Civil and Military Gazette," writing for the Indian press until about 1890, when he went to England, where he has lived ever since, with the exception of a short sojourn in America.

Even while he was still in India he achieved a popular as well as a literary success with his dramatic and skilful tales, sketches and ballads of Anglo-Indian life.

Soldiers Three (1888) was the first of six collections of short stories brought out in "Wheeler's Railway Library." They were followed by the far more sensitive and searching *Plain Tales from the Hills, Under the Deodars* and *The Phantom 'Rikshaw,* which contains two of the best and most convincing ghost-stories in recent literature.

These tales, however, display only one side of Kipling's extraordinary talents. As a writer of children's stories, he has few living equals. *Wee Willie Winkie,* which contains that stirring and heroic fragment "Drums of the Fore and Aft," is only a trifle less notable than his more obviously juvenile collections. *Just-So Stories* and the two *Jungle Books* (prose interspersed with lively rhymes) are classics for young people of all ages. *Kim,* the novel of a super-Mowgli grown up, is a more mature masterpiece.

Considered solely as a poet (see Preface) he is one of the most vigorous and unique figures of his time. The spirit of romance surges under his realities. His brisk lines conjure up the tang of a countryside in autumn, the tingle of salt spray, the rude sentiment of ruder natures, the snapping of a banner, the lurch and rumble of the sea. His poetry is woven of the stuff of myths; but it never loses its hold on actualities. Kipling himself in his poem "The Benefactors" (from *The Years Between* [1919]) writes:

> Ah! What avails the classic bent
> And what the cultured word,
> Against the undoctored incident
> That actually occurred?

Kipling won the Nobel Prize for Literature in 1907. His varied poems have finally been collected in a remarkable one-volume *Inclusive Edition* (1885-1918), an indispensable part of any student's library. This gifted and prolific creator, whose work was affected by the war, has frequently lapsed into bombast and a journalistic imperialism. At his best he is unforgettable, standing mountain-high above his host of imitators. His home is at Burwash, Sussex.

GUNGA DIN

> You may talk o' gin an' beer
> When you're quartered safe out 'ere,
> An' you're sent to penny-fights an' Aldershot it;
> But if it comes to slaughter
> You will do your work on water,
> An' you'll lick the bloomin' boots of 'im that's
>   got it.
> Now in Injia's sunny clime,
> Where I used to spend my time
> A-servin' of 'Er Majesty the Queen,
> Of all them black-faced crew
> The finest man I knew
> Was our regimental *bhisti*,[1] Gunga Din.

[1] The *bhisti*, or water-carrier, attached to regiments in India, is often one of the most devoted of the Queen's servants. He is also appreciated by the men.

It was " Din! Din! Din!
You limping lump o' brick-dust, Gunga
    Din!
Hi! *slippy hitherao!*
Water, get it! *Panee lao!*[1]
You squidgy-nosed old idol, Gunga Din!"

The uniform 'e wore
Was nothin' much before,
An' rather less than 'arf o' that be'ind,
For a twisty piece o' rag
An' a goatskin water-bag
Was all the field-equipment 'e could find.
When the sweatin' troop-train lay
In a sidin' through the day,
Where the 'eat would make your bloomin' eye-
      brows crawl,
We shouted *" Harry By!"*[2]
Till our throats were bricky-dry,
Then we wopped 'im 'cause 'e couldn't serve
      us all.

    It was "Din! Din! Din!
    You 'eathen, where the mischief 'ave you
      been?
    You put some *juldee*[3] in it,
    Or I'll *marrow*[4] you this minute,
    If you don't fill up my helmet, Gunga
      Din!"

[1] Bring water swiftly.
[2] Tommy Atkins' equivalent for " O Brother!"
[3] Speed.
[4] Hit you.

'E would dot an' carry one
Till the longest day was done,
An' 'e didn't seem to know the use o' fear.
If we charged or broke or cut,
You could bet your bloomin' nut,
'E'd be waitin' fifty paces right flank rear.
With 'is *mussick* [1] on 'is back,
'E would skip with our attack,
An' watch us till the bugles made " Retire."
An' for all 'is dirty 'ide,
'E was white, clear white, inside
When 'e went to tend the wounded under fire!

It was " Din! Din! Din! "
With the bullets kickin' dust-spots on
    the green.
When the cartridges ran out,
You could 'ear the front-files shout:
" Hi! ammunition-mules an' Gunga
    Din! "

I sha'n't forgit the night
When I dropped be'ind the fight
With a bullet where my belt-plate should
    'a' been.
I was chokin' mad with thirst,
An' the man that spied me first
Was our good old grinnin', gruntin' Gunga
    Din.

[1] Water-skin.

59

'E lifted up my 'ead,
An' 'e plugged me where I bled,
An' 'e guv me 'arf-a-pint o' water—green;
It was crawlin' an' it stunk,
But of all the drinks I've drunk,
I'm gratefullest to one from Gunga Din.

It was " Din! Din! Din!
'Ere's a beggar with a bullet through
    'is spleen;
'E's chawin' up the ground an' 'e's
    kickin' all around:
For Gawd's sake, git the water, Gunga
    Din! "

'E carried me away
To where a *dooli* lay,
An' a bullet come an' drilled the beggar clean.
'E put me safe inside,
An' just before 'e died:
" I 'ope you liked your drink," sez Gunga
        Din.
So I'll meet 'im later on
In the place where 'e is gone—
Where it's always double drill and no canteen;
'E'll be squattin' on the coals
Givin' drink to pore damned souls,
An' I'll get a swig in Hell from Gunga Din!

Rudyard Kipling

Din! Din! Din!
You Lazarushian-leather Gunga Din!
Tho' I've belted you an' flayed you,
By the livin' Gawd that made you,
You're a better man than I am, Gunga
    Din!

THE RETURN [1]

Peace is declared, and I return
    To 'Ackneystadt, but not the same;
Things 'ave transpired which made me learn
    The size and meanin' of the game.
I did no more than others did,
    I don't know where the change began;
I started as a average kid,
    I finished as a thinkin' man.

  If England was what England seems
    An' not the England of our dreams,
But only putty, brass, an' paint,
    'Ow quick we'd drop 'er! But she ain't!

Before my gappin' mouth could speak
    I 'eard it in my comrade's tone;
I saw it on my neighbour's cheek
    Before I felt it flush my own.

[1] From *The Five Nations* by Rudyard Kipling. Copyright by
Doubleday, Page & Co. and A. P. Watt & Son.

An' last it come to me—not pride,
  Nor yet conceit, but on the 'ole
(If such a term may be applied),
  The makin's of a bloomin' soul.

Rivers at night that cluck an' jeer,
  Plains which the moonshine turns to sea,
Mountains that never let you near,
  An' stars to all eternity;
An' the quick-breathin' dark that fills
  The 'ollows of the wilderness,
When the wind worries through the 'ills—
  These may 'ave taught me more or less.

Towns without people, ten times took,
  An' ten times left an' burned at last;
An' starvin' dogs that come to look
  For owners when a column passed;
An' quiet, 'omesick talks between
  Men, met by night, you never knew
Until—'is face—by shellfire seen—
  Once—an' struck off. They taught me, too.

The day's lay-out—the mornin' sun
  Beneath your 'at-brim as you sight;
The dinner-'ush from noon till one,
  An' the full roar that lasts till night;
An' the pore dead that look so old
  An' was so young an hour ago,
An' legs tied down before they're cold—
  These are the things which make you know.

Also Time runnin' into years—
   A thousand Places left be'ind—
An' Men from both two 'emispheres
   Discussin' things of every kind;
So much more near than I 'ad known,
   So much more great than I 'ad guessed—
An' me, like all the rest, alone—
   But reachin' out to all the rest!

So 'ath it come to me—not pride,
   Nor yet conceit, but on the 'ole
(If such a term may be applied),
   The makin's of a bloomin' soul.
But now, discharged, I fall away
   To do with little things again. . . .
Gawd, 'oo knows all I cannot say,
   Look after me in Thamesfontein!

If England was what England seems
   An' not the England of our dreams,
But only putty, brass, an' paint,
   'Ow quick we'd chuck 'er! But she ain't!

THE CONUNDRUM OF THE WORKSHOPS

When the flush of a newborn sun fell first on Eden's
   green and gold,
Our father Adam sat under the Tree and scratched with
   a stick in the mold;

63

And the first rude sketch that the world had seen was
joy to his mighty heart,
Till the Devil whispered behind the leaves: "It's pretty,
but is it Art?"

Wherefore he called to his wife and fled to fashion
his work anew—
The first of his race who cared a fig for the first, most
dread review;
And he left his lore to the use of his sons—and that was
a glorious gain
When the Devil chuckled: "Is it Art?" in the ear of
the branded Cain.

They builded a tower to shiver the sky and wrench the
stars apart,
Till the Devil grunted behind the bricks: "It's striking,
but is it Art?"
The stone was dropped by the quarry-side, and the idle
derrick swung,
While each man talked of the aims of art, and each in
an alien tongue.

They fought and they talked in the north and the south,
they talked and they fought in the west,
Till the waters rose on the jabbering land, and the poor
Red Clay had rest—
Had rest till the dank blank-canvas dawn when the dove
was preened to start,
And the Devil bubbled below the keel: "It's human, but
is it Art?"

Rudyard Kipling

The tale is old as the Eden Tree—as new as the new-
cut tooth—
For each man knows ere his lip-thatch grows he is
master of Art and Truth;
And each man hears as the twilight nears, to the beat of
his dying heart,
The Devil drum on the darkened pane: "You did it,
but was it Art?"

We have learned to whittle the Eden Tree to the shape
of a surplice-peg,
We have learned to bottle our parents twain in the yolk
of an addled egg,
We know that the tail must wag the dog, as the horse
is drawn by the cart;
But the Devil whoops, as he whooped of old: " It's clever,
but is it Art?"

When the flicker of London's sun falls faint on the club-
room's green and gold,
The sons of Adam sit them down and scratch with their
pens in the mold—
They scratch with their pens in the mold of their graves,
and the ink and the anguish start
When the Devil mutters behind the leaves: " It's pretty,
but is it art?"

Now, if we could win to the Eden Tree where the four
great rivers flow,
And the wreath of Eve is red on the turf as she left it
long ago,

And if we could come when the sentry slept, and softly
scurry through,
By the favor of God we might know as much—as our
father Adam knew.

AN ASTROLOGER'S SONG [1]

To the Heavens above us
O look and behold
The Planets that love us
All harnessed in gold!
What chariots, what horses
Against us shall bide
While the Stars in their courses
Do fight on our side?

All thought, all desires,
That are under the sun,
Are one with their fires,
As we also are one:
All matter, all spirit,
All fashion, all frame,
Receive and inherit
Their strength from the same.

(Oh, man that deniest
All power save thine own,
Their power in the highest
Is mightily shown.

---

[1] From *Rewards and Fairies* by Rudyard Kipling. Copyright by Doubleday, Page and Co. and A. P. Watt & Son.

66

Rudyard Kipling

Not less in the lowest
    That power is made clear.
Oh, man, if thou knowest,
    What treasure is here!)

Earth quakes in her throes
    And we wonder for why!
But the blind planet knows
    When her ruler is nigh;
And, attuned since Creation
    To perfect accord,
She thrills in her station
    And yearns to her Lord.

The waters have risen,
    The springs are unbound—
The floods break their prison,
    And ravin around.
No rampart withstands 'em,
    Their fury will last,
Till the Sign that commands 'em
    Sinks low or swings past.

Through abysses unproven
    And gulfs beyond thought,
Our portion is woven,
    Our burden is brought.
Yet They that prepare it,
    Whose Nature we share,
Make us who must bear it
    Well able to bear.

Rudyard Kipling

Though terrors o'ertake us
    We'll not be afraid.
No power can unmake us
    Save that which has made.
Nor yet beyond reason
    Or hope shall we fall—
All things have their season,
    And Mercy crowns all!

Then, doubt not, ye fearful—
    The Eternal is King—
Up, heart, and be cheerful,
    And lustily sing:—
What chariots, what horses
    Against us shall bide
While the Stars in their courses
    Do fight on our side?

Richard Le Gallienne

Richard Le Gallienne, who, in spite of his long residence in the United States, must be considered an English poet, was born at Liverpool in 1866. He entered on a business career soon after leaving Liverpool College, but gave up commercial life to become a man of letters after five or six years.

His early work was strongly influenced by the artificialities of the æsthetic movement (see Preface); the indebtedness to Oscar Wilde is especially evident. A little later Keats was the dominant influence, and *English Poems* (1892) betray how deep were Le Gallienne's admirations. His more recent poems in *The Lonely Dancer* (1913) show a keener individuality and a finer lyrical passion. His prose fancies are well known—par-

68

Richard Le Gallienne

ticularly *The Book Bills of Narcissus* and the charming and high-spirited fantasia, *The Quest of the Golden Girl*.

Le Gallienne came to America about 1905 and has lived ever since in Rowayton, Conn., and New York City.

A BALLAD OF LONDON

Ah, London! London! our delight,
Great flower that opens but at night,
Great City of the midnight sun,
Whose day begins when day is done.

Lamp after lamp against the sky
Opens a sudden beaming eye,
Leaping alight on either hand,
The iron lilies of the Strand.

Like dragonflies, the hansoms hover,
With jeweled eyes, to catch the lover;
The streets are full of lights and loves,
Soft gowns, and flutter of soiled doves.

The human moths about the light
Dash and cling close in dazed delight,
And burn and laugh, the world and wife,
For this is London, this is life!

Upon thy petals butterflies,
But at thy root, some say, there lies,
A world of weeping trodden things,
Poor worms that have not eyes or wings.

69

From out corruption of their woe
Springs this bright flower that charms us so,
Men die and rot deep out of sight
To keep this jungle-flower bright.

Paris and London, World-Flowers twain
Wherewith the World-Tree blooms again,
Since Time hath gathered Babylon,
And withered Rome still withers on.

Sidon and Tyre were such as ye,
How bright they shone upon the tree!
But Time hath gathered, both are gone,
And no man sails to Babylon.

REGRET

One asked of regret,
    And I made reply:
To have held the bird,
    And let it fly;
To have seen the star
    For a moment nigh,
And lost it
    Through a slothful eye;
To have plucked the flower
    And cast it by;
To have one only hope—
    To die.

Lionel Johnson

Born in 1867, Lionel Johnson received a classical education at Oxford, and his poetry is a faithful reflection of his studies in Greek and Latin literatures. Though he allied himself with the modern Irish poets, his Celtic origin is a literary myth; Johnson, having been converted to Catholicism in 1891, became imbued with Catholic and, later, with Irish traditions. His verse, while sometimes strained and over-decorated, is chastely designed, rich and, like that of the Cavalier poets of the sevententh century, mystically devotional. *Poems* (1895) contains his best work. Johnson died in 1902.

MYSTIC AND CAVALIER

Go from me: I am one of those who fall.
What! hath no cold wind swept your heart at all,
In my sad company? Before the end,
    Go from me, dear my friend!

Yours are the victories of light: your feet
Rest from good toil, where rest is brave and sweet:
But after warfare in a mourning gloom,
    I rest in clouds of doom.

Have you not read so, looking in these eyes?
Is it the common light of the pure skies,
Lights up their shadowy depths? The end is set:
    Though the end be not yet.

When gracious music stirs, and all is bright,
And beauty triumphs through a courtly night;
When I too joy, a man like other men:
    Yet, am I like them, then?

And in the battle, when the horsemen sweep
Against a thousand deaths, and fall on sleep:
Who ever sought that sudden calm, if I
      Sought not? yet could not die!

Seek with thine eyes to pierce this crystal sphere:
Canst read a fate there, prosperous and clear?
Only the mists, only the weeping clouds,
      Dimness and airy shrouds.

Beneath, what angels are at work? What powers
Prepare the secret of the fatal hours?
See! the mists tremble, and the clouds are stirred:
      When comes the calling word?

The clouds are breaking from the crystal ball,
Breaking and clearing: and I look to fall.
When the cold winds and airs of portent sweep,
      My spirit may have sleep.

O rich and sounding voices of the air!
Interpreters and prophets of despair:
Priests of a fearful sacrament! I come,
      To make with you mine home.

Lionel Johnson

TO A TRAVELLER

The mountains, and the lonely death at last
Upon the lonely mountains: O strong friend!
The wandering over, and the labour passed,
 Thou art indeed at rest:
 Earth gave thee of her best,
 That labour and this end.

Earth was thy mother, and her true son thou:
Earth called thee to a knowledge of her ways,
Upon the great hills, up the great streams: now
 Upon earth's kindly breast
 Thou art indeed at rest:
 Thou, and thine arduous days.

Fare thee well, O strong heart! The tranquil night
Looks calmly on thee: and the sun pours down
His glory over thee, O heart of might!
 Earth gives thee perfect rest:
 Earth, whom thy swift feet pressed:
 Earth, whom the vast stars crown.

Ernest Dowson

Ernest Dowson was born at Belmont Hill in Kent in 1867.
His great-uncle was Alfred Domett (Browning's "Waring"),
who was at one time Prime Minister of New Zealand. Dowson,
practically an invalid all his life, was reckless with himself

73

and, as disease weakened him more and more, hid himself in miserable surroundings; for almost two years he lived in sordid supper-houses known as "cabmen's shelters." He literally drank himself to death.

His delicate and fantastic poetry was an attempt to escape from a reality too big and brutal for him. His passionate lyric, "I have been faithful to thee, Cynara! in my fashion," a triumph of despair and disillusion, is an outburst in which Dowson epitomized himself—"One of the greatest lyrical poems of our time," writes Arthur Symons, "in it he has for once said everything, and he has said it to an intoxicating and perhaps immortal music."

Dowson died obscure in 1900, one of the finest of modern minor poets. His life was the tragedy of a weak nature buffeted by a strong and merciless environment.

TO ONE IN BEDLAM

With delicate, mad hands, behind his sordid bars,
Surely he hath his posies, which they tear and twine;
Those scentless wisps of straw that, miserable, line
His strait, caged universe, whereat the dull world stares.

Pedant and pitiful. O, how his rapt gaze wars
With their stupidity! Know they what dreams divine
Lift his long, laughing reveries like enchanted wine,
And make his melancholy germane to the stars'?

O lamentable brother! if those pity thee,
Am I not fain of all thy lone eyes promise me;
Half a fool's kingdom, far from men who sow and reap,
All their days, vanity? Better then mortal flowers,
Thy moon-kissed roses seem: better than love or sleep,
The star-crowned solitude of thine oblivious hours!

Ernest Dowson

YOU WOULD HAVE UNDERSTOOD ME

You would have understood me, had you waited;
    I could have loved you, dear! as well as he:
Had we not been impatient, dear! and fated
        Always to disagree.

What is the use of speech? Silence were fitter:
    Lest we should still be wishing things unsaid.
Though all the words we ever spake were bitter,
        Shall I reproach you, dead?

Nay, let this earth, your portion, likewise cover
    All the old anger, setting us apart:
Always, in all, in truth was I your lover;
        Always, I held your heart.

I have met other women who were tender,
    As you were cold, dear! with a grace as rare.
Think you, I turned to them, or made surrender,
        I who had found you fair?

Had we been patient, dear! ah, had you waited,
    I had fought death for you, better than he:
But from the very first, dear! we were fated
        Always to disagree.

Late, late, I come to you, now death discloses
    Love that in life was not to be our part:
On your low lying mound between the roses,
        Sadly I cast my heart.

75

Ernest Dowson

I would not waken you: nay! this is fitter;
    Death and the darkness give you unto me;
Here we who loved so, were so cold and bitter,
    Hardly can disagree.

" A. E."

(*George William Russell*)

At Durgan, a tiny town in the north of Ireland, George
William Russell was born in 1867. He moved to Dublin when
he was 10 years old and, as a young man, helped to form
the group that gave rise to the Irish Renascence—the group of
which William Butler Yeats, Doctor Douglas Hyde, Katharine
Tynan and Lady Gregory were brilliant members. Besides
being a splendid mystical poet, " A. E." is a painter of note,
a fiery patriot, a distinguished sociologist, a public speaker, a
student of economics and one of the heads of the Irish Agri-
cultural Association.

The best of his poetry is in *Homeward Songs by the Way*
(1894) and *The Earth Breath and Other Poems.* Yeats has
spoken of these poems as " revealing in all things a kind of
scented flame consuming them from within."

THE GREAT BREATH

Its edges foamed with amethyst and rose,
Withers once more the old blue flower of day:
There where the ether like a diamond glows,
    Its petals fade away.

A shadowy tumult stirs the dusky air;
Sparkle the delicate dews, the distant snows;
The great deep thrills—for through it everywhere
    The breath of Beauty blows.

76

"A. E."

I saw how all the trembling ages past,
Moulded to her by deep and deeper breath,
Near'd to the hour when Beauty breathes her last
And knows herself in death.

THE UNKNOWN GOD

Far up the dim twilight fluttered
    Moth-wings of vapour and flame:
The lights danced over the mountains,
    Star after star they came.

The lights grew thicker unheeded,
    For silent and still were we;
Our hearts were drunk with a beauty
    Our eyes could never see.

Stephen Phillips

Born in 1868, Stephen Phillips is best known as the author of
Herod (1900), *Paola and Francesca* (1899), and *Ulysses*
(1902); a poetic playwright who succeeded in reviving, for a
brief interval, the blank verse drama on the modern stage.
Hailed at first with extravagant and almost incredible praise,
Phillips lived to see his most popular dramas discarded and
his new ones, such as *Pietro of Siena* (1910), unproduced and
unnoticed.

Phillips failed to "restore" poetic drama because he was,
first of all, a lyric rather than a dramatic poet. In spite of
certain moments of rhetorical splendor, his scenes are spectacu-
lar instead of emotional; his inspiration is too often derived
from other models. He died in 1915.

77

Stephen Phillips

FRAGMENT FROM " HEROD "

Herod speaks:
I dreamed last night of a dome of beaten gold
To be a counter-glory to the Sun.
There shall the eagle blindly dash himself,
There the first beam shall strike, and there the moon
Shall aim all night her argent archery;
And it shall be the tryst of sundered stars,
The haunt of dead and dreaming Solomon;
Shall send a light upon the lost in Hell,
And flashings upon faces without hope.—
And I will think in gold and dream in silver,
Imagine in marble and conceive in bronze,
Till it shall dazzle pilgrim nations
And stammering tribes from undiscovered lands,
Allure the living God out of the bliss,
And all the streaming seraphim from heaven.

BEAUTIFUL LIE THE DEAD

Beautiful lie the dead;
   Clear comes each feature;
Satisfied not to be,
   Strangely contented.

Like ships, the anchor dropped,
   Furled every sail is;
Mirrored with all their masts
   In a deep water.

Stephen Phillips

A DREAM

My dead love came to me, and said:
　'God gives me one hour's rest,
To spend with thee on earth again:
　How shall we spend it best?'

'Why, as of old,' I said; and so
　We quarrelled, as of old:
But, when I turned to make my peace,
　That one short hour was told.

Laurence Binyon

Laurence Binyon was born at Lancaster, August 10, 1869, a
cousin of Stephen Phillips; in *Primavera* (1890) their early
poems appeared together. Binyon's subsequent volumes showed
little distinction until he published *London Visions*, which, in an
enlarged edition in 1908, revealed a gift of characterization
and a turn of speech in surprising contrast to his previous
academic *Lyrical Poems* (1894). His *Odes* (1901) contains his
ripest work; two poems in particular, "The Threshold" and
"The Bacchanal of Alexander," are glowing and unusually
spontaneous.

Binyon's power has continued to grow; age has given his
verse a new sharpness. "The House That Was," one of his
most recent poems, appeared in *The London Mercury*, Novem-
ber, 1919.

A SONG

For Mercy, Courage, Kindness, Mirth,
There is no measure upon earth.
Nay, they wither, root and stem,
If an end be set to them.

Overbrim and overflow,
If you own heart you would know;
For the spirit born to bless
Lives but in its own excess.

THE HOUSE THAT WAS

Of the old house, only a few crumbled
   Courses of brick, smothered in nettle and dock,
Or a squared stone, lying mossy where it tumbled!
   Sprawling bramble and saucy thistle mock
What once was firelit floor and private charm
   Where, seen in a windowed picture, hills were fading
At dusk, and all was memory-coloured and warm,
   And voices talked, secure from the wind's invading.

Of the old garden, only a stray shining
   Of daffodil flames amid April's cuckoo-flowers,
Or a cluster of aconite mixt with weeds entwining!
   But, dark and lofty, a royal cedar towers
By homely thorns: whether the white rain drifts
   Or sun scorches, he holds the downs in ken,
The western vale; his branchy tiers he lifts,
   Older than many a generation of men.

Alfred Douglas

Lord Alfred Douglas was born in 1870 and educated at
Magdalen College, Oxford. He was the editor of *The Academy* from 1907 to 1910 and was at one time the intimate friend

Alfred Douglas

of Oscar Wilde. One of the minor poets of "the eighteen-nineties," several of his poems rise above his own affectations and the end-of-the-century decadence. *The City of the Soul* (1899) and *Sonnets* (1900) contain his most graceful writing.

THE GREEN RIVER

I know a green grass path that leaves the field
    And, like a running river, winds along
    Into a leafy wood, where is no throng
Of birds at noon-day; and no soft throats yield
Their music to the moon. The place is sealed,
    An unclaimed sovereignty of voiceless song,
    And all the unravished silences belong
To some sweet singer lost, or unrevealed.

So is my soul become a silent place. . . .
    Oh, may I wake from this uneasy night
        To find some voice of music manifold.
Let it be shape of sorrow with wan face,
    Or love that swoons on sleep, or else delight
        That is as wide-eyed as a marigold.

T. Sturge Moore

Thomas Sturge Moore was born March 4, 1870. He is well known not only as an author, but as a critic and wood-engraver. As an artist, he has achieved no little distinction and has designed the covers for the poetry of W. B. Yeats and others. As a poet, the greater portion of his verse is severely classical in tone, academic in expression but, of its kind, dis-

T. Sturge Moore

tinctive and intimate. Among his many volumes, the most outstanding are *The Vinedresser and Other Poems* (1899), *A Sicilian Idyll* (1911) and *The Sea Is Kind* (1914).

THE DYING SWAN

O silver-throated Swan
Struck, struck! A golden dart
Clean through thy breast has gone
Home to thy heart.
Thrill, thrill, O silver throat!
O silver trumpet, pour
Love for defiance back
On him who smote!
And brim, brim o'er
With love; and ruby-dye thy track
Down thy last living reach
Of river, sail the golden light—
Enter the sun's heart—even teach
O wondrous-gifted Pain, teach Thou
The God of love, let him learn how!

SILENCE SINGS

So faint, no ear is sure it hears,
So faint and far;
So vast that very near appears
My voice, both here and in each star
Unmeasured leagues do bridge between;
Like that which on a face is seen
Where secrets are;

T. Sturge Moore

Sweeping, like veils of lofty balm,
Tresses unbound
O'er desert sand, o'er ocean calm,
I am wherever is not sound;
And, goddess of the truthful face,
My beauty doth instil its grace
That joy abound.

William H. Davies

According to his own biography, William H. Davies was
born in a public-house called Church House at Newport, in
the County of Monmouthshire, April 20, 1870, of Welsh parents.
He was, until Bernard Shaw "discovered" him, a cattleman, a
berry-picker, a panhandler—in short, a vagabond. In a preface
to Davies' second book, *The Autobiography of a Super-Tramp*
(1906), Shaw describes how the manuscript came into his
hands:

"In the year 1905 I received by post a volume of poems
by one William H. Davies, whose address was The Farm
House, Kensington, S. E. I was surprised to learn that there
was still a farmhouse left in Kensington; for I did not then
suspect that the Farm House, like the Shepherdess Walks and
Nightingale Lane and Whetstone Parks of Bethnal Green and
Holborn, is so called nowadays in irony, and is, in fact, a
doss-house, or hostelry, where single men can have a night's
lodging, for, at most, sixpence. . . . The author, as far as I
could guess, had walked into a printer's or stationer's shop;
handed in his manuscript; and ordered his book as he might
have ordered a pair of boots. It was marked 'price, half a
crown.' An accompanying letter asked me very civilly if I
required a half-crown book of verses; and if so, would I
please send the author the half crown: if not, would I return
the book. This was attractively simple and sensible. I opened

83

the book, and was more puzzled than ever; for before I had read three lines I perceived that the author was a real poet. His work was not in the least strenuous or modern; there was indeed no sign of his ever having read anything otherwise than as a child reads. . . . Here, I saw, was a genuine innocent, writing odds and ends of verse about odds and ends of things; living quite out of the world in which such things are usually done, and knowing no better (or rather no worse) than to get his book made by the appropriate craftsman and hawk it round like any other ware."

It is more than likely that Davies' first notoriety as a tramp-poet who had ridden the rails in the United States and had had his right foot cut off by a train in Canada, obscured his merits as a genuine singer. Even his early *The Soul's Destroyer* (1907) revealed that simplicity which is as *naïf* as it is strange. The volumes that followed are more clearly melodious, more like the visionary wonder of Blake, more artistically artless.

With the exception of "The Villain," which has not yet appeared in book form, the following poems are taken from *The Collected Poems of W. H. Davies* (1916) with the permission of the publisher, Alfred A. Knopf.

DAYS TOO SHORT

When primroses are out in Spring,
   And small, blue violets come between;
   When merry birds sing on boughs green,
And rills, as soon as born, must sing;

When butterflies will make side-leaps,
   As though escaped from Nature's hand
   Ere perfect quite; and bees will stand
Upon their heads in fragrant deeps;

84

William H. Davies

When small clouds are so silvery white
  Each seems a broken rimmèd moon—
  When such things are, this world too soon,
For me, doth wear the veil of Night.

THE MOON

Thy beauty haunts me heart and soul,
  Oh, thou fair Moon, so close and bright;
Thy beauty makes me like the child
  That cries aloud to own thy light:
The little child that lifts each arm
To press thee to her bosom warm.

Though there are birds that sing this night
  With thy white beams across their throats,
Let my deep silence speak for me
  More than for them their sweetest notes:
Who worships thee till music fails,
Is greater than thy nightingales.

THE VILLAIN

While joy gave clouds the light of stars,
  That beamed where'er they looked;
And calves and lambs had tottering knees,
  Excited, while they sucked;

William H. Davies

While every bird enjoyed his song,
Without one thought of harm or wrong—
I turned my head and saw the wind,
   Not far from where I stood,
Dragging the corn by her golden hair,
   Into a dark and lonely wood.

THE EXAMPLE

Here's an example from
   A Butterfly;
That on a rough, hard rock
   Happy can lie;
Friendless and all alone
On this unsweetened stone.

Now let my bed be hard,
   No care take I;
I'll make my joy like this
   Small Butterfly;
Whose happy heart has power
To make a stone a flower.

Hilaire Belloc

Hilaire Belloc, who has been described as " a Frenchman, an Englishman, an Oxford man, a country gentleman, a soldier, a satirist, a democrat, a novelist, and a practical journalist," was born July 27, 1870. After leaving school he served as a driver in the 8th Regiment of French Artillery at Toul Meurthe-et-Moselle, being at that time a French citizen. He was naturalized as a British subject somewhat later, and in 1906 he entered the House of Commons as Liberal Member for South Salford.

As an author, he has engaged in multiple activities. He has written three satirical novels, one of which, *Mr. Clutterbuck's Election,* sharply exposes British newspapers and underground politics. His *Path to Rome* (1902) is a high-spirited and ever-delightful travel book which has passed through many editions. His historical studies and biographies of *Robespierre* and *Marie Antoinette* (1909) are classics of their kind. As a poet he is only somewhat less engaging. His *Verses* (1910) is a rather brief collection of poems on a wide variety of themes. Although his humorous and burlesque stanzas are refreshing, Belloc is most himself when he writes either of malt liquor or his beloved Sussex. Though his religious poems are full of a fine romanticism, "The South Country" is the most pictorial and persuasive of his serious poems. His poetic as well as his spiritual kinship with G. K. Chesterton is obvious.

THE SOUTH COUNTRY

When I am living in the Midlands
    That are sodden and unkind,
I light my lamp in the evening:
    My work is left behind;
And the great hills of the South Country
    Come back into my mind.

The great hills of the South Country
    They stand along the sea;
And it's there walking in the high woods
    That I could wish to be,
And the men that were boys when I was a boy
    Walking along with me.

Hilaire Belloc

The men that live in North England
    I saw them for a day:
Their hearts are set upon the waste fells,
    Their skies are fast and grey;
From their castle-walls a man may see
    The mountains far away.

The men that live in West England
    They see the Severn strong,
A-rolling on rough water brown
    Light aspen leaves along.
They have the secret of the Rocks,
    And the oldest kind of song.

But the men that live in the South Country
    Are the kindest and most wise,
They get their laughter from the loud surf,
    And the faith in their happy eyes
Comes surely from our Sister the Spring
    When over the sea she flies;
The violets suddenly bloom at her feet,
    She blesses us with surprise.

I never get between the pines
    But I smell the Sussex air;
Nor I never come on a belt of sand
    But my home is there.
And along the sky the line of the Downs
    So noble and so bare.

Hilaire Belloc

A lost thing could I never find,
    Nor a broken thing mend:
And I fear I shall be all alone
    When I get towards the end.
Who will there be to comfort me
    Or who will be my friend?

I will gather and carefully make my friends
    Of the men of the Sussex Weald;
They watch the stars from silent folds,
    They stiffly plough the field.
By them and the God of the South Country
    My poor soul shall be healed.

If I ever become a rich man,
    Or if ever I grow to be old,
I will build a house with deep thatch
    To shelter me from the cold,
And there shall the Sussex songs be sung
    And the story of Sussex told.

I will hold my house in the high wood
    Within a walk of the sea,
And the men that were boys when I was a boy
    Shall sit and drink with me.

Anthony C. Deane

Anthony C. Deane was born in 1870 and was the Seatonian
prizeman in 1905 at Clare College, Cambridge. He has been
Vicar of All Saints, Ennismore Gardens, since 1916. His long

list of light verse and essays includes several excellent paro-
dies, the most delightful being found in his *New Rhymes for
Old* (1901).

THE BALLAD OF THE *BILLYCOCK*

It was the good ship *Billycock,* with thirteen men aboard,
  Athirst to grapple with their country's foes,—
A crew, 'twill be admitted, not numerically fitted
  To navigate a battleship in prose.

It was the good ship *Billycock* put out from Plymouth
    Sound,
  While lustily the gallant heroes cheered,
And all the air was ringing with the merry bo'sun's sing-
    ing,
  Till in the gloom of night she disappeared.

But when the morning broke on her, behold, a dozen
    ships,
  A dozen ships of France around her lay,
(Or, if that isn't plenty, I will gladly make it twenty),
  And hemmed her close in Salamander Bay.

Then to the Lord High Admiral there spake a cabin-boy:
  "Methinks," he said, "the odds are somewhat great,
And, in the present crisis, a cabin-boy's advice is
  That you and France had better arbitrate!"

"Pooh!" said the Lord High Admiral, and slapped his
    manly chest,
"Pooh! That would be both cowardly and wrong;
Shall I, a gallant fighter, give the needy ballad-writer
    No suitable material for song?"

"Nay—is the shorthand-writer here?—I tell you, one and
    all,
    I mean to do my duty, as I ought;
With eager satisfaction let us clear the decks for action
    And fight the craven Frenchmen!" So they fought.

And (after several stanzas which as yet are incomplete,
    Describing all the fight in epic style)
When the *Billycock* was going, she'd a dozen prizes
    towing
    (Or twenty, as above) in single file!

Ah, long in glowing English hearts the story will remain,
    The memory of that historic day,
And, while we rule the ocean, we will picture with
    emotion
    The *Billycock* in Salamander Bay!

P.S.—I've lately noticed that the critics—who, I think,
    In praising *my* productions are remiss—
Quite easily are captured, and profess themselves en-
    raptured,
    By patriotic ditties such as this,

For making which you merely take some dauntless Eng-
lishmen,
  Guns, heroism, slaughter, and a fleet—
Ingredients you mingle in a metre with a jingle,
  And there you have your masterpiece complete!

Why, then, with labour infinite, produce a book of verse
  To languish on the " All for Twopence " shelf?
The ballad bold and breezy comes particularly easy—
  I mean to take to writing it myself!

A RUSTIC SONG

Oh, I be vun of the useful troibe
  O' rustic volk, I be;
And writin' gennelmen dü descroibe
  The doin's o' such as we;
I don't knaw mooch o' corliflower plants,
  I can't tell 'oes from trowels,
But 'ear me mix ma consonants,
  An' moodle oop all ma vowels!

I talks in a wunnerful dialect
  That vew can hunderstand,
'Tis Yorkshire-Zummerzet, I expect,
  With a dash o' the Oirish brand;
Sometimes a bloomin' flower of speech
  I picks from Cockney spots,
And when releegious truths I teach,
  Obsairve ma richt gude Scots!

In most of the bukes, 'twas once the case
  I 'adn't got much to do,
I blessed the 'eroine's purty face,
  An' I seëd the 'ero through;
But now, I'm juist a pairsonage!
  A power o' bukes there be
Which from the start to the very last page
  Entoirely deal with me!

The wit or the point o' what I spakes
  Ye've got to find if ye can;
A wunnerful difference spellin' makes
  In the 'ands of a competent man!
I mayn't knaw mooch o' corliflower plants,
  I mayn't knaw 'oes from trowels,
But I does ma wark, if ma consonants
  Be properly mixed with ma vowels!

J. M. Synge

The most brilliant star of the Celtic revival was born at
Rathfarnham, near Dublin, in 1871. As a child in Wicklow,
he was already fascinated by the strange idioms and the rhyth-
mic speech he heard there, a native utterance which was his
greatest delight and which was to be rich material for his great-
est work. He did not use this folk-language merely as he
heard it. He was an artist first and last, and as an artist
he bent and shaped the rough material, selecting with great
fastidiousness, so that in his plays every speech is, as he himself
declared all good speech should be, " as fully flavored as a
nut or apple." Even in *The Tinker's Wedding* (1907), pos-

sibly the least important of his plays, one is arrested by snatches like:

> "That's a sweet tongue you have, Sarah Casey; but if sleep's a grand thing, it's a grand thing to be waking up a day the like of this, when there's a warm sun in it, and a kind air, and you'll hear the cuckoos singing and crying out on the top of the hill."

For some time, Synge's career was uncertain. He went to Germany half intending to become a professional musician. There he studied the theory of music, perfecting himself meanwhile in Gaelic and Hebrew, winning prizes in both of these languages. Yeats found him in France in 1898 and advised him to go to the Aran Islands, to live there as if he were one of the people. "Express a life," said Yeats, "that has never found expression." Synge went. He became part of the life of Aran, living upon salt fish and eggs, talking Irish for the most part but listening also to that beautiful English which, to quote Yeats again, "has grown up in Irish-speaking districts and takes its vocabulary from the time of Malory and of the translators of the Bible, but its idiom and vivid metaphor from Irish." The result of this close contact was five of the greatest poetic prose dramas not only of his own generation, but of several generations preceding it. (See Preface.)

In *Riders to the Sea* (1903), *The Well of the Saints* (1905), and *The Playboy of the Western World* (1907) we have a richness of imagery, a new language startling in its vigor, a wildness and passion that contrast strangely with the suave mysticism and delicate spirituality of his associates in the Irish Theatre.

Synge's *Poems and Translations* (1910), a volume which was not issued until after his death, contains not only his few hard and earthy verses, but also Synge's theory of poetry. The translations, which have been rendered in a highly intensified prose, are as racy as anything in his plays; his versions of Villon and Petrarch are remarkable for their adherence to the original and still radiate the poet's own personality.

Synge died, just as he was beginning to attain fame, at a private hospital in Dublin March 24, 1909.

J. M. Synge

BEG-INNISH

Bring Kateen-beug and Maurya Jude
To dance in Beg-Innish,[1]
And when the lads (they're in Dunquin)
Have sold their crabs and fish,
Wave fawny shawls and call them in,
And call the little girls who spin,
And seven weavers from Dunquin,
To dance in Beg-Innish.

I'll play you jigs, and Maurice Kean,
Where nets are laid to dry,
I've silken strings would draw a dance
From girls are lame or shy;
Four strings I've brought from Spain and
    France
To make your long men skip and prance,
Till stars look out to see the dance
Where nets are laid to dry.

We'll have no priest or peeler in
To dance in Beg-Innish;
But we'll have drink from M'riarty Jim
Rowed round while gannets fish,
A keg with porter to the brim,
That every lad may have his whim,
Till we up sails with M'riarty Jim
And sail from Beg-Innish.

[1] (The accent is on the last syllable.)

J. M. Synge

A TRANSLATION FROM PETRARCH

(He is Jealous of the Heavens and the Earth)

What a grudge I am bearing the earth that has its arms
about her, and is holding that face away from me, where
I was finding peace from great sadness.

What a grudge I am bearing the Heavens that are
after taking her, and shutting her in with greediness, the
Heavens that do push their bolt against so many.

What a grudge I am bearing the blessed saints that
have got her sweet company, that I am always seeking;
and what a grudge I am bearing against Death, that is
standing in her two eyes, and will not call me with a
word.

TO THE OAKS OF GLENCREE

My arms are round you, and I lean
Against you, while the lark
Sings over us, and golden lights, and green
Shadows are on your bark.

There'll come a season when you'll stretch
Black boards to cover me;
Then in Mount Jerome I will lie, poor wretch,
With worms eternally.

Nora Hopper Chesson

Nora Hopper was born in Exeter on January 2, 1871, and married W. H. Chesson, a well-known writer, in 1901. Although the Irish element in her work is acquired and incidental, there is a distinct if somewhat fitful race consciousness in *Ballads in Prose* (1894) and *Under Quickened Boughs* (1896). She died suddenly April 14, 1906.

A CONNAUGHT LAMENT

I will arise and go hence to the west,
And dig me a grave where the hill-winds call;
But O were I dead, were I dust, the fall
Of my own love's footstep would break my rest!

My heart in my bosom is black as a sloe!
I heed not cuckoo, nor wren, nor swallow:
Like a flying leaf in the sky's blue hollow
The heart in my breast is, that beats so low.

Because of the words your lips have spoken,
(O dear black head that I must not follow)
My heart is a grave that is stripped and hollow,
As ice on the water my heart is broken.

O lips forgetful and kindness fickle,
The swallow goes south with you: I go west
Where fields are empty and scythes at rest.
I am the poppy and you the sickle;
My heart is broken within my breast.

Eva Gore-Booth

Eva Gore-Booth, the second daughter of Sir Henry Gore-Booth and the sister of Countess Marcievicz, was born in Sligo, Ireland, in 1872. She first appeared in " A. E." 's anthology, *New Songs,* in which so many of the modern Irish poets first came forward.

Her initial volume, *Poems* (1898), showed practically no distinction—not even the customary " promise." But *The One and the Many* (1904) and *The Sorrowful Princess* (1907) revealed the gift of the Celtic singer who is half mystic, half minstrel. Primarily philosophic, her verse often turns to lyrics as haunting as the two examples here reprinted.

THE WAVES OF BREFFNY

The grand road from the mountain goes shining to the
    sea,
  And there is traffic on it and many a horse and cart,
But the little roads of Cloonagh are dearer far to me
  And the little roads of Cloonagh go rambling through
    my heart.

A great storm from the ocean goes shouting o'er the hill,
  And there is glory in it; and terror on the wind:
But the haunted air of twilight is very strange and still,
  And the little winds of twilight are dearer to my mind.

The great waves of the Atlantic sweep storming on their
    way,
  Shining green and silver with the hidden herring shoal;
But the little waves of Breffny have drenched my heart
    in spray,
  And the little waves of Breffny go stumbling through
    my soul.

Eva Gore-Booth

WALLS

Free to all souls the hidden beauty calls,
The sea thrift dwelling on her spray-swept height,
The lofty rose, the low-grown aconite,
The gliding river and the stream that brawls
Down the sharp cliffs with constant breaks and falls—
All these are equal in the equal light—
All waters mirror the one Infinite.

God made a garden, it was men built walls;
But the wide sea from men is wholly freed;
Freely the great waves rise and storm and break,
Nor softlier go for any landlord's need,
Where rhythmic tides flow for no miser's sake
And none hath profit of the brown sea-weed,
But all things give themselves, yet none may take.

Moira O'Neill

Moira O'Neill is known chiefly by a remarkable little collection of only twenty-five lyrics, *Songs from the Glens of Antrim* (1900), simple tunes as unaffected as the peasants of whom she sings. The best of her poetry is dramatic without being theatrical; melodious without falling into the tinkle of most "popular" sentimental verse.

A BROKEN SONG

'*Where am I from?*' From the green hills of Erin.
'*Have I no song then?*' My songs are all sung.
'*What o' my love?*' 'Tis alone I am farin'.
Old grows my heart, an' my voice yet is young.

'*If she was tall?*' Like a king's own daughter.
'*If she was fair?*' Like a mornin' o' May.
When she'd come laughin' 'twas the runnin' wather,
When she'd come blushin' 'twas the break o' day.

'*Where did she dwell?*' Where one'st I had my dwellin'.
'*Who loved her best?*' There's no one now will know.
'*Where is she gone?*' Och, why would I be tellin'!
Where she is gone there I can never go.

BEAUTY'S A FLOWER

> *Youth's for an hour,*
> *Beauty's a flower,*
> *But love is the jewel that wins the world.*

Youth's for an hour, an' the taste o' life is sweet,
Ailes was a girl that stepped on two bare feet;
In all my days I never seen the one as fair as she,
I'd have lost my life for Ailes, an' she never cared for me.

Beauty's a flower, an' the days o' life are long,
There's little knowin' who may live to sing another song;
For Ailes was the fairest, but another is my wife,
An' Mary—God be good to her!—is all I love in life.

> *Youth's for an hour,*
> *Beauty's a flower,*
> *But love is the jewel that wins the world.*

John McCrae

John McCrae was born in Guelph, Ontario, Canada, in 1872.
He was graduated in arts in 1894 and in medicine in 1898. He
finished his studies at Johns Hopkins in Baltimore and returned
to Canada, joining the staff of the Medical School of McGill
University. He was a lieutenant of artillery in South Africa
(1899-1900) and was in charge of the Medical Division of the
McGill Canadian General Hospital during the World War.
After serving two years, he died of pneumonia, January, 1918,
his volume *In Flanders Fields* (1919) appearing posthumously.

Few who read the title poem of his book, possibly the most
widely-read poem produced by the war, realize that it is a
perfect rondeau, one of the loveliest (and strictest) of the
French forms.

IN FLANDERS FIELDS

In Flanders fields the poppies blow
Between the crosses, row on row,
   That mark our place; and in the sky
   The larks, still bravely singing, fly
Scarce heard amid the guns below.

We are the Dead. Short days ago
We lived, felt dawn, saw sunset glow,
   Loved and were loved, and now we lie
      In Flanders fields.

Take up our quarrel with the foe:
To you from failing hands we throw
   The torch; be yours to hold it high.
   If ye break faith with us who die
We shall not sleep, though poppies grow
      In Flanders fields.

Ford Madox Hueffer

Ford Madox Hueffer was born in 1873 and is best known as the author of many novels, two of which, *Romance* and *The Inheritors*, were written in collaboration with Joseph Conrad. He has written also several critical studies, those on Rossetti and Henry James being the most notable. His *On Heaven and Other Poems* appeared in 1916.

CLAIR DE LUNE

I

I should like to imagine
A moonlight in which there would be no machine-
    guns!

For, it is possible
To come out of a trench or a hut or a tent or a
    church all in ruins:
To see the black perspective of long avenues
All silent.
The white strips of sky
At the sides, cut by the poplar trunks:
The white strips of sky
Above, diminishing—
The silence and blackness of the avenue
Enclosed by immensities of space
Spreading away
Over No Man's Land. . . .

For a minute . . .
For ten . . .
There will be no star shells
But the untroubled stars,

Ford Madox Hueffer

There will be no *Very* light
But the light of the quiet moon
Like a swan.
And silence. . . .

Then, far away to the right thro' the moonbeams
"*Wukka Wukka*" will go the machine-guns,
And, far away to the left
Wukka Wukka.
And sharply,
Wuk . . . *Wuk* . . . and then silence
For a space in the clear of the moon.

II

I should like to imagine
A moonlight in which the machine-guns of trouble
Will be silent. . . .

Do you remember, my dear,
Long ago, on the cliffs, in the moonlight,
Looking over to Flatholme
We sat . . . Long ago! . . .
And the things that you told me . . .
Little things in the clear of the moon,
The little, sad things of a life. . . .

We shall do it again
Full surely,
Sitting still, looking over at Flatholme.

Then, far away to the right
Shall sound the Machine Guns of trouble
Wukka-wukka!
And, far away to the left, under Flatholme,
Wukka-wuk! . . .

            .

I wonder, my dear, can you stick it?
As we should say: "Stick it, the Welch!"
In the dark of the moon,
Going over. . . .

"THERE SHALL BE MORE JOY . . ."

The little angels of Heaven
Each wear a long white dress,
And in the tall arcadings
Play ball and play at chess;

With never a soil on their garments,
Not a sigh the whole day long,
Not a bitter note in their pleasure,
Not a bitter note in their song.

But they shall know keener pleasure,
And they shall know joy more rare—
Keener, keener pleasure
When you, my dear, come there.

.   .   .   .   .

Ford Madox Hueffer

The little angels of Heaven
Each wear a long white gown,
And they lean over the ramparts
Waiting and looking down.

Walter De la Mare

The author of some of the most haunting lyrics in contemporary poetry, Walter De la Mare, was born in 1873. Although he did not begin to bring out his work in book form until he was over 30, he is, as Harold Williams has written, "the singer of a young and romantic world, a singer even for children, understanding and perceiving as a child." De la Mare paints simple scenes of miniature loveliness; he uses thin-spun fragments of fairy-like delicacy and achieves a grace that is remarkable in its universality. "In a few words, seemingly artless and unsought" (to quote Williams again), "he can express a pathos or a hope as wide as man's life."

De la Mare is an astonishing joiner of words; in *Peacock Pie* (1913) he surprises us again and again by transforming what began as a child's nonsense-rhyme into a suddenly thrilling snatch of music. A score of times he takes things as casual as the feeding of chickens or the swallowing of physic, berry-picking, eating, hair-cutting—and turns them into magic. These poems read like lyrics of William Shakespeare rendered by Mother Goose. The trick of revealing the ordinary in whimsical colors, of catching the commonplace off its guard, is the first of De la Mare's two magics.

This poet's second gift is his sense of the supernatural, of the fantastic other-world that lies on the edges of our consciousness. *The Listeners* (1912) is a book that, like all the best of De la Mare, is full of half-heard whispers; moonlight and mystery seem soaked in the lines, and a cool wind from Nowhere blows over them. That most magical of modern verses, "The Listeners," and the brief music of "An Epitaph" are two fine examples among many. In the first of these poems there is an uncanny splendor. What we have here is the effect, the thrill, the overtones of a ghost story rather than the narrative itself—the less than half-told adventure of some new Childe Roland heroically challenging a heedless universe. Never have silence and black night been reproduced more creepily, nor has the symbolism of man's courage facing the cryptic riddle of life been more memorably expressed.

De la Mare's chief distinction, however, lies not so much in what he says as in how he says it; he can even take outworn words like "thridding," "athwart," "amaranthine" and make them live again in a poetry that is of no time and of all time. He writes, it has been said, as much for antiquity as for posterity; he is a poet who is distinctively in the world and yet not wholly of it.

THE LISTENERS

'Is there anybody there?' said the Traveller,
    Knocking on the moonlit door;
And his horse in the silence champed the grasses
    Of the forest's ferny floor.
And a bird flew up out of the turret,
    Above the Traveller's head:
And he smote upon the door again a second time;
    'Is there anybody there?' he said.
But no one descended to the Traveller;
    No head from the leaf-fringed sill
Leaned over and looked into his grey eyes,
    Where he stood perplexed and still.
But only a host of phantom listeners
    That dwelt in the lone house then
Stood listening in the quiet of the moonlight
    To that voice from the world of men:

Stood thronging the faint moonbeams on the dark
    stair,
  That goes down to the empty hall,
Hearkening in an air stirred and shaken
  By the lonely Traveller's call.
And he felt in his heart their strangeness,
  Their stillness answering his cry,
While his horse moved, cropping the dark turf,
  'Neath the starred and leafy sky;
For he suddenly smote on the door, even
  Louder, and lifted his head:—
'Tell them I came, and no one answered,
  That I kept my word,' he said.
Never the least stir made the listeners,
  Though every word he spake
Fell echoing through the shadowiness of the still
    house
  From the one man left awake:
Ay, they heard his foot upon the stirrup,
  And the sound of iron on stone,
And how the silence surged softly backward,
  When the plunging hoofs were gone.

AN EPITAPH

  Here lies a most beautiful lady,
  Light of step and heart was she;
  I think she was the most beautiful lady
  That ever was in the West Country.

But beauty vanishes; beauty passes;
However rare—rare it be;
And when I crumble, who will remember
This lady of the West Country?

TIRED TIM

Poor tired Tim! It's sad for him.
He lags the long bright morning through,
Ever so tired of nothing to do;
He moons and mopes the livelong day,
Nothing to think about, nothing to say;
Up to bed with his candle to creep,
Too tired to yawn; too tired to sleep:
Poor tired Tim! It's sad for him.

OLD SUSAN

When Susan's work was done, she'd sit
With one fat guttering candle lit,
And window opened wide to win
The sweet night air to enter in;
There, with a thumb to keep her place
She'd read, with stern and wrinkled face.
Her mild eyes gliding very slow
Across the letters to and fro,
While wagged the guttering candle flame
In the wind that through the window came.

And sometimes in the silence she
Would mumble a sentence audibly,
Or shake her head as if to say,
'You silly souls, to act this way!'
And never a sound from night I'd hear,
Unless some far-off cock crowed clear;
Or her old shuffling thumb should turn
Another page; and rapt and stern,
Through her great glasses bent on me
She'd glance into reality;
And shake her round old silvery head,
With—'You!—I thought you was in bed!'—
Only to tilt her book again,
And rooted in Romance remain.

NOD

Softly along the road of evening,
    In a twilight dim with rose,
Wrinkled with age, and drenched with dew
    Old Nod, the shepherd, goes.

His drowsy flock streams on before him,
    Their fleeces charged with gold,
To where the sun's last beam leans low
    On Nod the shepherd's fold.

The hedge is quick and green with briar,
    From their sand the conies creep;
And all the birds that fly in heaven
    Flock singing home to sleep.

Walter De la Mare

His lambs outnumber a noon's roses,
    Yet, when night's shadows fall,
His blind old sheep-dog, Slumber-soon,
    Misses not one of all.

His are the quiet steeps of dreamland,
    The waters of no-more-pain;
His ram's bell rings 'neath an arch of stars,
    " Rest, rest, and rest again."

G. K. Chesterton

This brilliant journalist, novelist, essayist, publicist and lyricist, Gilbert Keith Chesterton, was born at Campden Hill, Kensington, in 1874, and began his literary life by reviewing books on art for various magazines. He is best known as a writer of flashing, paradoxical essays on anything and everything, like *Tremendous Trifles* (1909), *Varied Types* (1905), and *All Things Considered* (1910). But he is also a stimulating critic; a keen appraiser, as in his volume *Heretics* (1905) and his analytical studies of Robert Browning, Charles Dickens, and George Bernard Shaw; a writer of strange and grotesque romances like *The Napoleon of Notting Hill* (1906), *The Man Who Was Thursday* (1908), which Chesterton himself has subtitled "A Nightmare," and *The Flying Inn* (1914); the author of several books of fantastic short stories, ranging from the wildly whimsical narratives in *The Club of Queer Trades* (1905) to that amazing sequence *The Innocence of Father Brown* (1911)—which is a series of religious detective stories!

Besides being the creator of all of these, Chesterton finds time to be a prolific if sometimes too acrobatic newspaperman, a lay preacher in disguise (witness *Orthodoxy* [1908], *What's Wrong with the World?* [1910], *The Ball and the Cross*

G. K. Chesterton

[1909]) a pamphleteer, and a poet. His first volume of verse, *The Wild Knight and Other Poems* (1900), a collection of quaintly-flavored and affirmative verses, was followed by *The Ballad of the White Horse* (1911), one long poem which, in spite of Chesterton's ever-present didactic sermonizing, is possibly the most stirring creation he has achieved. This poem has the swing, the vigor, the spontaneity, and, above all, the ageless simplicity of the true narrative ballad.

Scarcely less notable is the ringing "Lepanto" from his later *Poems* (1915) which, anticipating the banging, clanging verses of Vachel Lindsay's "The Congo," is one of the finest of modern chants. It is interesting to see how the syllables beat, as though on brass; it is thrilling to feel how, in one's pulses, the armies sing, the feet tramp, the drums snarl, and all the tides of marching crusaders roll out of lines like:

"Strong gongs groaning as the guns boom far,
Don John of Austria is going to the war;
Stiff flags straining in the night-blasts cold
In the gloom black-purple, in the glint old-gold;
Torchlight crimson on the copper kettle-drums,
Then the tuckets, then the trumpets, then the cannon, and he
  comes. . . ."

Chesterton, the prose-paradoxer, is a delightful product of a skeptical age. But it is Chesterton the poet who is more likely to outlive it.

LEPANTO [1]

White founts falling in the Courts of the sun,
And the Soldan of Byzantium is smiling as they run;
There is laughter like the fountains in that face of all
    men feared,
It stirs the forest darkness, the darkness of his beard;

---

[1] From *Poems* by G. K. Chesterton. Copyright by the John Lane Co. and reprinted by permission of the publishers.

It curls the blood-red crescent, the crescent of his lips;
For the inmost sea of all the earth is shaken with his ships.
They have dared the white republics up the capes of
    Italy,
They have dashed the Adriatic round the Lion of the Sea,
And the Pope has cast his arms abroad for agony and
    loss,
And called the kings of Christendom for swords about
    the Cross.
The cold queen of England is looking in the glass;
The shadow of the Valois is yawning at the Mass;
From evening isles fantastical rings faint the Spanish gun,
And the Lord upon the Golden Horn is laughing in the
    sun.

Dim drums throbbing, in the hills half heard,
Where only on a nameless throne a crownless prince has
    stirred,
Where, risen from a doubtful seat and half attainted stall,
The last knight of Europe takes weapons from the wall,
The last and lingering troubadour to whom the bird has
    sung,
That once went singing southward when all the world
    was young.
In that enormous silence, tiny and unafraid,
Comes up along a winding road the noise of the Crusade.
Strong gongs groaning as the guns boom far,
Don John of Austria is going to the war,
Stiff flags straining in the night-blasts cold
In the gloom black-purple, in the glint old-gold,

Torchlight crimson on the copper kettle-drums,
Then the tuckets, then the trumpets, then the cannon,
    and he comes.
Don John laughing in the brave beard curled,
Spurning of his stirrups like the thrones of all the world,
Holding his head up for a flag of all the free.
Love-light of Spain—hurrah!
Death-light of Africa!
Don John of Austria
Is riding to the sea.

Mahound is in his paradise above the evening star,
(*Don John of Austria is going to the war.*)
He moves a mighty turban on the timeless houri's knees,
His turban that is woven of the sunsets and the seas.
He shakes the peacock gardens as he rises from his ease,
And he strides among the tree-tops and is taller than the
    trees;
And his voice through all the garden is a thunder sent to
    bring
Black Azrael and Ariel and Ammon on the wing.
Giants and the Genii,
Multiplex of wing and eye,
Whose strong obedience broke the sky
When Solomon was king.

They rush in red and purple from the red clouds of the
    morn,
From the temples where the yellow gods shut up their
    eyes in scorn;

They rise in green robes roaring from the green hells of
the sea

Where fallen skies and evil hues and eyeless crea-
tures be,

On them the sea-valves cluster and the grey sea-forests
curl,

Splashed with a splendid sickness, the sickness of the
pearl;

They swell in sapphire smoke out of the blue cracks of
the ground,—

They gather and they wonder and give worship to
Mahound.

And he saith, "Break up the mountains where the her-
mit-folk can hide,

And sift the red and silver sands lest bone of saint
abide,

And chase the Giaours flying night and day, not giving
rest,

For that which was our trouble comes again out of the
west.

We have set the seal of Solomon on all things under sun,

Of knowledge and of sorrow and endurance of things
done.

But a noise is in the mountains, in the mountains, and I
know

The voice that shook our palaces—four hundred years
ago:

It is he that saith not 'Kismet'; it is he that knows not
Fate;

It is Richard, it is Raymond, it is Godfrey at the gate!

G. K. Chesterton

It is he whose loss is laughter when he counts the wager
    worth,
Put down your feet upon him, that our peace be on the
    earth."
For he heard drums groaning and he heard guns jar,
(*Don John of Austria is going to the war.*)
Sudden and still—hurrah!
Bolt from Iberia!
Don John of Austria
Is gone by Alcalar.

St. Michael's on his Mountain in the sea-roads of the
    north
(*Don John of Austria is girt and going forth.*)
Where the grey seas glitter and the sharp tides shift
And the sea-folk labour and the red sails lift.
He shakes his lance of iron and he claps his wings of
    stone;
The noise is gone through Normandy; the noise is gone
    alone;
The North is full of tangled things and texts and aching
    eyes,
And dead is all the innocence of anger and surprise,
And Christian killeth Christian in a narrow dusty room,
And Christian dreadeth Christ that hath a newer face
    of doom,
And Christian hateth Mary that God kissed in Galilee,—
But Don John of Austria is riding to the sea.
Don John calling through the blast and the eclipse
Crying with the trumpet, with the trumpet of his lips,

G. K. Chesterton

Trumpet that sayeth *ha!*
> *Domino gloria!*

Don John of Austria
Is shouting to the ships.

King Philip's in his closet with the Fleece about his neck
(*Don John of Austria is armed upon the deck.*)
The walls are hung with velvet that is black and soft
> as sin,

And little dwarfs creep out of it and little dwarfs creep in.
He holds a crystal phial that has colours like the moon,
He touches, and it tingles, and he trembles very soon,
And his face is as a fungus of a leprous white and grey
Like plants in the high houses that are shuttered from
> the day,

And death is in the phial and the end of noble work,
But Don John of Austria has fired upon the Turk.
Don John's hunting, and his hounds have bayed—
Booms away past Italy the rumour of his raid.
Gun upon gun, ha! ha!
Gun upon gun, hurrah!
Don John of Austria
Has loosed the cannonade.

The Pope was in his chapel before day or battle broke,
(*Don John of Austria is hidden in the smoke.*)
The hidden room in man's house where God sits all the
> year,

The secret window whence the world looks small and
> very dear.

G. K. Chesterton

He sees as in a mirror on the monstrous twilight sea
The crescent of his cruel ships whose name is mystery;
They fling great shadows foe-wards, making Cross and
      Castle dark,
They veil the plumèd lions on the galleys of St. Mark;
And above the ships are palaces of brown, black-bearded
      chiefs,
And below the ships are prisons, where with multitudi-
      nous griefs,
Christian captives sick and sunless, all a labouring race
      repines
Like a race in sunken cities, like a nation in the mines.
They are lost like slaves that sweat, and in the skies of
      morning hung
The stair-ways of the tallest gods when tyranny was
      young.
They are countless, voiceless, hopeless as those fallen or
      fleeing on
Before the high Kings' horses in the granite of Babylon.
And many a one grows witless in his quiet room in hell
Where a yellow face looks inward through the lattice of
      his cell,
And he finds his God forgotten, and he seeks no more a
      sign—
(*But Don John of Austria has burst the battle-line!*)
Don John pounding from the slaughter-painted poop,
Purpling all the ocean like a bloody pirate's sloop,
Scarlet running over on the silvers and the golds,
Breaking of the hatches up and bursting of the holds,
Thronging of the thousands up that labour under sea
White for bliss and blind for sun and stunned for liberty.

G. K. Chesterton

Vivat Hispania!
Domino Gloria!
Don John of Austria
Has set his people free!

Cervantes on his galley sets the sword back in the sheath
(*Don John of Austria rides homeward with a wreath.*)
And he sees across a weary land a straggling road in
      Spain,
Up which a lean and foolish knight for ever rides in vain,
And he smiles, but not as Sultans smile, and settles back
      the blade. . . .
(*But Don John of Austria rides home from the Crusade.*)

A PRAYER IN DARKNESS

This much, O heaven—if I should brood or rave,
   Pity me not; but let the world be fed,
   Yea, in my madness if I strike me dead,
Heed you the grass that grows upon my grave.

If I dare snarl between this sun and sod,
   Whimper and clamour, give me grace to own,
   In sun and rain and fruit in season shown,
The shining silence of the scorn of God.

Thank God the stars are set beyond my power,
   If I must travail in a night of wrath,
   Thank God my tears will never vex a moth,
Nor any curse of mine cut down a flower.

G. K. Chesterton

Men say the sun was darkened: yet I had
    Thought it beat brightly, even on—Calvary:
And He that hung upon the Torturing Tree
Heard all the crickets singing, and was glad.

THE DONKEY

" The tattered outlaw of the earth,
    Of ancient crooked will;
Starve, scourge, deride me: I am dumb,
    I keep my secret still.

" Fools! For I also had my hour;
    One far fierce hour and sweet:
There was a shout about my ears,
    And palms before my feet."

Wilfrid Wilson Gibson

Born at Hexam in 1878, Wilfrid Wilson Gibson has published
almost a dozen books of verse—the first four or five (see
Preface) being imitative in manner and sentimentally romantic
in tone. With *The Stonefolds* (1907) and *Daily Bread* (1910),
Gibson executed a complete right-about-face and, with dra-
matic brevity, wrote a series of poems mirroring the dreams,
pursuits and fears of common humanity. *Fires* (1912) marks
an advance in technique and power. And though in *Liveli-
hood* (1917) Gibson seems to be theatricalizing and merely
exploiting his working-people, his later lyrics recapture the
veracity of such memorable poems as " The Old Man," " The

119

Wilfrid Wilson Gibson

Blind Rower," and "The Machine." *Hill-Tracks* (1918) attempts to capture the beauty of village-names and the glamour of the English countryside.

PRELUDE

As one, at midnight, wakened by the call
Of golden-plovers in their seaward flight,
Who lies and listens, as the clear notes fall
Through tingling silence of the frosty night—
Who lies and listens, till the last note fails,
And then, in fancy, faring with the flock
Far over slumbering hills and dreaming dales,
Soon hears the surges break on reef and rock;
And, hearkening, till all sense of self is drowned
Within the mightier music of the deep,
No more remembers the sweet piping sound
That startled him from dull, undreaming sleep;
So I, first waking from oblivion, heard,
With heart that kindled to the call of song,
The voice of young life, fluting like a bird,
And echoed that light lilting; till, ere long,
Lured onward by that happy, singing-flight,
I caught the stormy summons of the sea,
And dared the restless deeps that, day and night,
Surge with the life-song of humanity.

Wilfrid Wilson Gibson

THE STONE [1]

" And will you cut a stone for him,
To set above his head?
And will you cut a stone for him—
A stone for him?" she said.

Three days before, a splintered rock
Had struck her lover dead—
Had struck him in the quarry dead,
Where, careless of the warning call,
He loitered, while the shot was fired—
A lively stripling, brave and tall,
And sure of all his heart desired . . .
A flash, a shock,
A rumbling fall . . .
And, broken 'neath the broken rock,
A lifeless heap, with face of clay;
And still as any stone he lay,
With eyes that saw the end of all.

I went to break the news to her;
And I could hear my own heart beat
With dread of what my lips might say
But, some poor fool had sped before;
And flinging wide her father's door,
Had blurted out the news to her,

[1] From *Fires* by Wilfrid Wilson Gibson. Copyright, 1912, by
The Macmillan Co. Reprinted by permission of the publishers.

Had struck her lover dead for her,
Had struck the girl's heart dead in her,
Had struck life, lifeless, at a word,
And dropped it at her feet:
Then hurried on his witless way,
Scarce knowing she had heard.

And when I came, she stood, alone
A woman, turned to stone:
And, though no word at all she said,
I knew that all was known.

Because her heart was dead,
She did not sigh nor moan,
His mother wept:
She could not weep.
Her lover slept:
She could not sleep.
Three days, three nights,
She did not stir:
Three days, three nights,
Were one to her,
Who never closed her eyes
From sunset to sunrise,
From dawn to evenfall:
Her tearless, staring eyes,
That seeing naught, saw all.

The fourth night when I came from work,
I found her at my door.
" And will you cut a stone for him? "
She said: and spoke no more:

But followed me, as I went in,
And sank upon a chair;
And fixed her grey eyes on my face,
With still, unseeing stare.
And, as she waited patiently,
I could not bear to feel
Those still, grey eyes that followed me,
Those eyes that plucked the heart from me,
Those eyes that sucked the breath from me
And curdled the warm blood in me,
Those eyes that cut me to the bone,
And pierced my marrow like cold steel.

And so I rose, and sought a stone;
And cut it, smooth and square:
And, as I worked, she sat and watched,
Beside me, in her chair.
Night after night, by candlelight,
I cut her lover's name:
Night after night, so still and white,
And like a ghost she came;
And sat beside me in her chair;
And watched with eyes aflame.

She eyed each stroke;
And hardly stirred:
She never spoke
A single word:
And not a sound or murmur broke
The quiet, save the mallet-stroke.

123

Wilfrid Wilson Gibson

With still eyes ever on my hands,
With eyes that seemed to burn my hands,
My wincing, overwearied hands,
She watched, with bloodless lips apart,
And silent, indrawn breath:
And every stroke my chisel cut,
Death cut still deeper in her heart:
The two of us were chiselling,
Together, I and death.

And when at length the job was done,
And I had laid the mallet by,
As if, at last, her peace were won,
She breathed his name; and, with a sigh,
Passed slowly hrough the open door:
And never crossed my threshold more.

Next night I laboured late, alone,
To cut her name upon the stone.

SIGHT [1]

By the lamplit stall I loitered, feasting my eyes
On colours ripe and rich for the heart's desire—
Tomatoes, redder than Krakatoa's fire,

[1] From *Borderlands and Thoroughfares* by Wilfrid Wilson Gibson. Copyright, 1915, by The Macmillan Company. Reprinted by permission of the publishers.

Wilfrid Wilson Gibson

Oranges like old sunsets over Tyre,
And apples golden-green as the glades of Paradise.

And as I lingered, lost in divine delight,
My heart thanked God for the goodly gift of sight
And all youth's lively senses keen and quick . . .
When suddenly, behind me in the night,
I heard the tapping of a blind man's stick.

John Masefield

John Masefield was born June 1, 1878, in Ledbury, Hertfordshire. He was the son of a lawyer but, being of a restless disposition, he took to the sea at an early age and became a wanderer for several years. At one time, in 1895, to be exact, he worked for a few months as a sort of third assistant barkeeper and dish-washer in Luke O'Connor's saloon, the Columbia Hotel, in New York City. The place is still there on the corner of Sixth and Greenwich Avenues.

The results of his wanderings showed in his early works, *Salt-Water Ballads* (1902), *Ballads* (1903), frank and often crude poems of sailors written in their own dialect, and *A Mainsail Haul* (1905), a collection of short nautical stories. In these books Masefield possibly overemphasized passion and brutality but, underneath the violence, he captured that highly-colored realism which is the poetry of life.

It was not until he published *The Everlasting Mercy* (1911) that he became famous. Followed quickly by those remarkable long narrative poems, *The Widow in the Bye Street* (1912), *Dauber* (1912), and *The Daffodil Fields* (1913), there is in all of these that peculiar blend of physical exulting and spiritual exaltation that is so striking, and so typical of Masefield. Their very rudeness is lifted to a plane of religious intensity. (See Preface.) Pictorially, Masefield is even more forceful. The finest moment in *The Widow in the Bye Street* is the por-

John Masefield

trayal of the mother alone in her cottage; the public-house scene and the passage describing the birds following the plough are the most intense touches in *The Everlasting Mercy*. Nothing more vigorous and thrilling than the description of the storm at sea in *Dauber* has appeared in current literature.

The war, in which Masefield served with the Red Cross in France and on the Gallipoli peninsula (of which campaign he wrote a study for the government), softened his style; *Good Friday and Other Poems* (1916) is as restrained and dignified a collection as that of any of his contemporaries. *Reynard the Fox* (1919) is the best of his new manner with a return of the old vivacity.

Masefield has also written several novels of which *Multitude and Solitude* (1909) is the most outstanding; half a dozen plays, ranging from the classical solemnity of *Pompey the Great* to the hot and racy *Tragedy of Nan;* and one of the freshest, most creative critiques of *Shakespeare* (1911) in the last generation.

A CONSECRATION

Not of the princes and prelates with periwigged
    charioteers
Riding triumphantly laurelled to lap the fat of the
    years,—
Rather the scorned—the rejected—the men hemmed in
    with the spears;

The men of the tattered battalion which fights till it dies,
Dazed with the dust of the battle, the din and the cries.
The men with the broken heads and the blood running
    into their eyes.

Not the be-medalled Commander, beloved of the throne,
Riding cock-horse to parade when the bugles are blown,
But the lads who carried the koppie and cannot be known.

Not the ruler for me, but the ranker, the tramp of the
    road,
The slave with the sack on his shoulders pricked on with
    the goad,
The man with too weighty a burden, too weary a load.

The sailor, the stoker of steamers, the man with the clout,
The chantyman bent at the halliards putting a tune to
    the shout,
The drowsy man at the wheel and the tired look-out.

Others may sing of the wine and the wealth and the
    mirth,
The portly presence of potentates goodly in girth;—
Mine be the dirt and the dross, the dust and scum of the
    earth!

Theirs be the music, the colour, the glory, the gold;
Mine be a handful of ashes, a mouthful of mould.
Of the maimed, of the halt and the blind in the rain and
    the cold—
Of these shall my songs be fashioned, my tales be told.
AMEN.

SEA-FEVER

I must down to the seas again, to the lonely sea and the
    sky,
And all I ask is a tall ship and a star to steer her by,
And the wheel's kick and the wind's song and the white
    sail's shaking,
And a grey mist on the sea's face and a grey dawn
    breaking.

John Masefield

I must down to the seas again, for the call of the running
    tide
Is a wild call and a clear call that may not be denied;
And all I ask is a windy day with the white clouds flying,
And the flung spray and the blown spume, and the sea-
    gulls crying.

I must down to the seas again to the vagrant gypsy life,
To the gull's way and the whale's way where the wind's
    like a whetted knife;
And all I ask is a merry yarn from a laughing fellow-
    rover,
And quiet sleep and a sweet dream when the long trick's
    over.

ROUNDING THE HORN

(From "Dauber")[1]

Then came the cry of "Call all hands on deck!"
The Dauber knew its meaning; it was come:
Cape Horn, that tramples beauty into wreck,
And crumples steel and smites the strong man dumb.
Down clattered flying kites and staysails; some
Sang out in quick, high calls: the fair-leads skirled,
And from the south-west came the end of the
    world . . .

[1] From *The Story of a Round-House* by John Masefield.
Copyright, 1913, by The Macmillan Company. Reprinted by
permission of the publishers.

"Lay out!" the Bosun yelled. The Dauber laid
Out on the yard, gripping the yard, and feeling
Sick at the mighty space of air displayed
Below his feet, where mewing birds were wheeling.
A giddy fear was on him; he was reeling.
He bit his lip half through, clutching the jack.
A cold sweat glued the shirt upon his back.

The yard was shaking, for a brace was loose.
He felt that he would fall; he clutched, he bent,
Clammy with natural terror to the shoes
While idiotic promptings came and went.
Snow fluttered on a wind-flaw and was spent;
He saw the water darken. Someone yelled,
"Frap it; don't stay to furl! Hold on!" He held.

Darkness came down—half darkness—in a whirl;
The sky went out, the waters disappeared.
He felt a shocking pressure of blowing hurl
The ship upon her side. The darkness speared
At her with wind; she staggered, she careered;
Then down she lay. The Dauber felt her go,
He saw her yard tilt downwards. Then the snow

Whirled all about—dense, multitudinous, cold—
Mixed with the wind's one devilish thrust and shriek,
Which whiffled out men's tears, defeated, took hold,
Flattening the flying drift against the cheek.
The yards buckled and bent, man could not speak.
The ship lay on her broadside; the wind's sound
Had devilish malice at having got her downed.

.   .   .   .

John Masefield

How long the gale had blown he could not tell,
Only the world had changed, his life had died.
A moment now was everlasting hell.
Nature an onslaught from the weather side,
A withering rush of death, a frost that cried,
Shrieked, till he withered at the heart; a hail
Plastered his oilskins with an icy mail. . . .

"Up!" yelled the Bosun; "up and clear the wreck!"
The Dauber followed where he led; below
He caught one giddy glimpsing of the deck
Filled with white water, as though heaped with snow.
He saw the streamers of the rigging blow
Straight out like pennons from the splintered mast,
Then, all sense dimmed, all was an icy blast.

Roaring from nether hell and filled with ice,
Roaring and crashing on the jerking stage,
An utter bridle given to utter vice,
Limitless power mad with endless rage
Withering the soul; a minute seemed an age.
He clutched and hacked at ropes, at rags of sail,
Thinking that comfort was a fairy tale,

Told long ago—long, long ago—long since
Heard of in other lives—imagined, dreamed—
There where the basest beggar was a prince.
To him in torment where the tempest screamed,
Comfort and warmth and ease no longer seemed
Things that a man could know; soul, body, brain,
Knew nothing but the wind, the cold, the pain.

John Masefield

THE CHOICE

The Kings go by with jewelled crowns;
Their horses gleam, their banners shake,
  their spears are many.
The sack of many-peopled towns
Is all their dream:
The way they take
Leaves but a ruin in the brake,
And, in the furrow that the ploughmen make,
A stampless penny; a tale, a dream.

The Merchants reckon up their gold,
Their letters come, their ships arrive, their
   freights are glories:
The profits of their treasures sold
They tell and sum;
Their foremen drive
Their servants, starved to half-alive,
Whose labours do but make the earth a hive
Of stinking glories; a tale, a dream.

The Priests are singing in their stalls,
Their singing lifts, their incense burns,
  their praying clamours;
Yet God is as the sparrow falls,
The ivy drifts;
The votive urns
Are all left void when Fortune turns,
The god is but a marble for the kerns
To break with hammers; a tale, a dream.

John Masefield

O Beauty, let me know again
The green earth cold, the April rain, the
    quiet waters figuring sky,
The one star risen.
So shall I pass into the feast
Not touched by King, Merchant, or Priest;
Know the red spirit of the beast,
Be the green grain;
Escape from prison.

SONNET [1]

Is there a great green commonwealth of Thought
Which ranks the yearly pageant, and decides
How Summer's royal progress shall be wrought,
By secret stir which in each plant abides?
Does rocking daffodil consent that she,
The snowdrop of wet winters, shall be first?
Does spotted cowslip with the grass agree
To hold her pride before the rattle burst?
And in the hedge what quick agreement goes,
When hawthorn blossoms redden to decay,
That Summer's pride shall come, the Summer's rose,
Before the flower be on the bramble spray?
Or is it, as with us, unresting strife,
And each consent a lucky gasp for life?

[1] From *Good Friday and Other Poems* by John Masefield. Copyright, 1916, by The Macmillan Company. Reprinted by permission of the publishers.

Lord Dunsany

Edward John Moreton Drax Plunkett, Lord Dunsany, was born July 24, 1878, and was educated at Eton and Sandhurst. He is best known as an author of fantastic fairy tales and even more fantastic plays. *The Gods of the Mountain* (1911) and *The Golden Doom* (1912) are highly dramatic and intensely poetic. *A Night at an Inn* (1916) is that peculiar novelty, an eerie and poetical melodrama.

Dunsany's prime quality is a romantic and highly colored imagination which is rich in symbolism. After the World War, in which the playwright served as captain in the Royal Inniskilling Fusiliers, Dunsany visited America and revised the reissue of his early tales and prose poems collected in his *The Book of Wonder*.

SONGS FROM AN EVIL WOOD

I

There is no wrath in the stars,
    They do not rage in the sky;
I look from the evil wood
    And find myself wondering why,

Why do they not scream out
    And grapple star against star,
Seeking for blood in the wood
    As all things round me are?

They do not glare like the sky
    Or flash like the deeps of the wood;
But they shine softly on
    In their sacred solitude.

133

Lord Dunsany

To their high, happy haunts
  Silence from us has flown,
She whom we loved of old
  And know it now she is gone.

When will she come again,
  Though for one second only?
She whom we loved is gone
  And the whole world is lonely.

And the elder giants come
  Sometimes, tramping from far
Through the weird and flickering light
  Made by an earthly star.

And the giant with his club,
  And the dwarf with rage in his breath,
And the elder giants from far,
  They are all the children of Death.

They are all abroad to-night
  And are breaking the hills with their
      brood,—
And the birds are all asleep
  Even in Plug Street Wood!

II

Somewhere lost in the haze
  The sun goes down in the cold,
And birds in this evil wood
  Chirrup home as of old;

Lord Dunsany

Chirrup, stir and are still,
  On the high twigs frozen and thin.
There is no more noise of them now,
  And the long night sets in.

Of all the wonderful things
  That I have seen in the wood
I marvel most at the birds
  And their wonderful quietude.

For a giant smites with his club
  All day the tops of the hill,
Sometimes he rests at night,
  Oftener he beats them still.

And a dwarf with a grim black mane
  Raps with repeated rage
All night in the valley below
  On the wooden walls of his cage.

III

I met with Death in his country,
  With his scythe and his hollow eye,
Walking the roads of Belgium.
  I looked and he passed me by.

Since he passed me by in Plug Street,
  In the wood of the evil name,
I shall not now lie with the heroes,
  I shall not share their fame;

Lord Dunsany

I shall never be as they are,
A name in the lands of the Free,
Since I looked on Death in Flanders
And he did not look at me.

Edward Thomas

Edward Thomas, one of the little-known but most individual
of modern English poets, was born in 1878. For many years
before he turned to verse, Thomas had a large following as a
critic and author of travel books, biographies, pot-boilers.
Hating his hack-work, yet unable to get free of it, he had so
repressed his creative ability that he had grown doubtful con-
cerning his own power. It needed something foreign to stir
and animate what was native in him. So when Robert Frost,
the New England poet, went abroad in 1912 for two years and
became an intimate of Thomas's, the English critic began to
write poetry. Loving, like Frost, the *minutiæ* of existence, the
quaint and casual turn of ordinary life, he caught the magic
of the English countryside in its unpoeticized quietude. Many
of his poems are full of a slow, sad contemplation of life and
a reflection of its brave futility. It is not disillusion exactly;
it is rather an absence of illusion. *Poems* (1917), dedicated to
Robert Frost, is full of Thomas's fidelity to little things, things
as unglorified as the unfreezing of the " rock-like mud," a
child's path, a list of quaint-sounding villages, birds' nests
uncovered by the autumn wind, dusty nettles—the lines glow
with a deep and almost abject reverence for the soil.

Thomas was killed at Arras, at an observatory outpost, on
Easter Monday, 1917.

IF I SHOULD EVER BY CHANCE

If I should ever by chance grow rich   2-
I'll buy Codham, Cockridden, and Childerditch,
Roses, Pyrgo, and Lapwater,
And let them all to my elder daughter.

Edward Thomas

The rent I shall ask of her will be only
Each year's first violets, white and lonely,
The first primroses and orchises—
She must find them before I do, that is.
But if she finds a blossom on furze
Without rent they shall all for ever be hers,
Codham, Cockridden, and Childerditch,
Roses, Pyrgo and Lapwater,—
I shall give them all to my elder daughter.

TALL NETTLES

Tall nettles cover up, as they have done
These many springs, the rusty harrow, the plough
Long worn out, and the roller made of stone:
Only the elm butt tops the nettles now.

This corner of the farmyard I like most:
As well as any bloom upon a flower
I like the dust on the nettles, never lost
Except to prove the sweetness of a shower.

FIFTY FAGGOTS

There they stand, on their ends, the fifty faggots
That once were underwood of hazel and ash
In Jenny Pinks's Copse. Now, by the hedge
Close packed, they make a thicket fancy alone

Edward Thomas

Can creep through with the mouse and wren. Next
Spring
A blackbird or a robin will nest there,
Accustomed to them, thinking they will remain
Whatever is for ever to a bird.
This Spring it is too late; the swift has come,
'Twas a hot day for carrying them up:
Better they will never warm me, though they must
Light several Winters' fires. Before they are done
The war will have ended, many other things
Have ended, maybe, that I can no more
Foresee or more control than robin and wren.

COCK-CROW

Out of the wood of thoughts that grows by night
To be cut down by the sharp axe of light,—
Out of the night, two cocks together crow,
Cleaving the darkness with a silver blow:
And bright before my eyes twin trumpeters stand,
Heralds of splendour, one at either hand,
Each facing each as in a coat of arms:—
The milkers lace their boots up at the farms.

Seumas O'Sullivan

James Starkey was born in Dublin in 1879. Writing under
the pseudonym of Seumas O'Sullivan, he contributed a great
variety of prose and verse to various Irish papers. His repu-

138

tation as a poet began with his appearance in *New Songs,* edited by George Russell (" A. E."). Later, he published *The Twilight People* (1905), *The Earth Lover* (1909), and *Poems* (1912).

PRAISE

Dear, they are praising your beauty,
The grass and the sky:
The sky in a silence of wonder,
The grass in a sigh.

I too would sing for your praising,
Dearest, had I
Speech as the whispering grass,
Or the silent sky.

These have an art for the praising
Beauty so high.
Sweet, you are praised in a silence,
Sung in a sigh.

Ralph Hodgson

This exquisite poet was born in Northumberland about 1879. One of the most graceful of the younger word-magicians, Ralph Hodgson will retain his freshness as long as there are lovers of such rare and timeless songs as his. It is difficult to think of any anthology of English poetry compiled after 1917 that could omit " Eve," " The Song of Honor," and that memorable snatch of music, " Time, You Old Gypsy Man." One succumbs to the charm of " Eve " at the first reading; for here is the

oldest of all legends told with a surprising simplicity and
still more surprising freshness. This Eve is neither the con-
scious sinner nor the Mother of men; she is, in Hodgson's
candid lines, any young, English country girl—filling her
basket, regarding the world and the serpent itself with a mild
and childlike wonder.

Hodgson's verses, full of the love of all natural things, a
love that goes out to

> "an idle rainbow
> No less than laboring seas,"

were originally brought out in small pamphlets, and distributed
by *Flying Fame.*

EVE

Eve, with her basket, was
Deep in the bells and grass,
Wading in bells and grass
Up to her knees.
Picking a dish of sweet
Berries and plums to eat,
Down in the bells and grass
Under the trees.

Mute as a mouse in a
Corner the cobra lay,
Curled round a bough of the
Cinnamon tall. . . .
Now to get even and
Humble proud heaven and
Now was the moment or
Never at all.

Ralph Hodgson

"Eva!" Each syllable
Light as a flower fell,
"Eva!" he whispered the
Wondering maid,
Soft as a bubble sung
Out of a linnet's lung,
Soft and most silverly
"Eva!" he said.

Picture that orchard sprite;
Eve, with her body white,
Supple and smooth to her
Slim finger tips;
Wondering, listening,
Listening, wondering,
Eve with a berry
Half-way to her lips.

Oh, had our simple Eve
Seen through the make-believe!
Had she but known the
Pretender he was!
Out of the boughs he came,
Whispering still her name,
Tumbling in twenty rings
Into the grass.

Here was the strangest pair
In the world anywhere,
Eve in the bells and grass
Kneeling, and he

Telling his story low. . . .
Singing birds saw them go
Down the dark path to
The Blasphemous Tree.

Oh, what a clatter when
Titmouse and Jenny Wren
Saw him successful and
Taking his leave!
How the birds rated him,
How they all hated him!
How they all pitied
Poor motherless Eve!

Picture her crying
Outside in the lane,
Eve, with no dish of sweet
Berries and plums to eat,
Haunting the gate of the
Orchard in vain. . . .
Picture the lewd delight
Under the hill to-night—
" Eva! " the toast goes round,
" Eva! " again.

TIME, YOU OLD GIPSY MAN

Time, you old gipsy man,
  Will you not stay,
Put up your caravan
  Just for one day?

Ralph Hodgson

All things I'll give you
Will you be my guest,
Bells for your jennet
Of silver the best,
Goldsmiths shall beat you
A great golden ring,
Peacocks shall bow to you,
Little boys sing,
Oh, and sweet girls will
Festoon you with may.
Time, you old gipsy,
Why hasten away?

Last week in Babylon,
Last night in Rome,
Morning, and in the crush
Under Paul's dome;
Under Paul's dial
You tighten your rein—
Only a moment,
And off once again;
Off to some city
Now blind in the womb,
Off to another
Ere that's in the tomb.

Time, you old gipsy man,
 Will you not stay,
Put up your caravan
 Just for one day?

Ralph Hodgson

THE BIRDCATCHER

When flighting time is on, I go
With clap-net and decoy,
A-fowling after goldfinches
And other birds of joy;

I lurk among the thickets of
The Heart where they are bred,
And catch the twittering beauties as
They fly into my Head.

THE MYSTERY

He came and took me by the hand
   Up to a red rose tree,
He kept His meaning to Himself
   But gave a rose to me.

I did not pray Him to lay bare
   The mystery to me,
Enough the rose was Heaven to smell,
   And His own face to see.

Harold Monro

The publisher of the various anthologies of Georgian Poetry, Harold Monro, was born in Brussels in 1879. He describes himself as " author, publisher, editor and book-seller." Monro

144

Harold Monro

founded The Poetry Bookshop in London in 1912, a unique establishment having as its object a practical relation between poetry and the public, and keeping in stock nothing but poetry, the drama, and books connected with these subjects. His quarterly *Poetry and Drama* (discontinued during the war and revived in 1919 as *The Monthly Chapbook*), was in a sense the organ of the younger men; and his shop, in which he has lived for the last seven years except while he was in the army, became a genuine literary center.

Of Monro's books, the two most important are *Strange Meetings* (1917) and *Children of Love* (1919). "The Nightingale Near the House," one of the loveliest of his poems, is also one of his latest and has not yet appeared in any of his volumes.

THE NIGHTINGALE NEAR THE HOUSE

Here is the soundless cypress on the lawn:
It listens, listens. Taller trees beyond
Listen. The moon at the unruffled pond
    Stares. And you sing, you sing.

That star-enchanted song falls through the air
From lawn to lawn down terraces of sound,
Darts in white arrows on the shadowed ground;
    And all the night you sing.

My dreams are flowers to which you are a bee
As all night long I listen, and my brain
Receives your song; then loses it again
    In moonlight on the lawn.

Now is your voice a marble high and white,
Then like a mist on fields of paradise,
Now is a raging fire, then is like ice,
    Then breaks, and it is dawn.

Harold Monro

EVERY THING

Since man has been articulate,
Mechanical, improvidently wise,
(Servant of Fate),
He has not understood the little cries
And foreign conversations of the small
Delightful creatures that have followed him
Not far behind;
Has failed to hear the sympathetic call
Of Crockery and Cutlery, those kind
Reposeful Teraphim
Of his domestic happiness; the Stool
He sat on, or the Door he entered through:
He has not thanked them, overbearing fool!
What is he coming to?

But you should listen to the talk of these.
Honest they are, and patient they have kept;
Served him without his Thank you or his
        Please . . .
I often heard
The gentle Bed, a sigh between each word,
Murmuring, before I slept.
The Candle, as I blew it, cried aloud,
Then bowed,
And in a smoky argument
Into the darkness went.

Harold Monro

The Kettle puffed a tentacle of breath:—
"Pooh! I have boiled his water, I don't know
Why; and he always says I boil too slow.
He never calls me "Sukie, dear," and oh,
I wonder why I squander my desire
Sitting submissive on his kitchen fire."

Now the old Copper Basin suddenly
Rattled and tumbled from the shelf,
Bumping and crying: "I can fall by myself;
Without a woman's hand
To patronize and coax and flatter me,
I understand
The lean and poise of gravitable land."
It gave a raucous and tumultuous shout,
Twisted itself convulsively about,
Rested upon the floor, and, while I stare,
It stares and grins at me.

The old impetuous Gas above my head
Begins irascibly to flare and fret,
Wheezing into its epileptic jet,
Reminding me I ought to go to bed.

The Rafters creak; an Empty-Cupboard door
Swings open; now a wild Plank of the floor
Breaks from its joist, and leaps behind my foot.
Down from the chimney, half a pound of Soot
Tumbles and lies, and shakes itself again.
The Putty cracks against the window-pane.

Harold Monro

A piece of Paper in the basket shoves
Another piece, and toward the bottom moves.
My independent Pencil, while I write,
Breaks at the point: the ruminating Clock
Stirs all its body and begins to rock,
Warning the waiting presence of the Night,
Strikes the dead hour, and tumbles to the plain
Ticking of ordinary work again.

You do well to remind me, and I praise
Your strangely individual foreign ways.
You call me from myself to recognize
Companionship in your unselfish eyes.
I want your dear acquaintances, although
I pass you arrogantly over, throw
Your lovely sounds, and squander them along
My busy days. I'll do you no more wrong.

Purr for me, Sukie, like a faithful cat.
You, my well trampled Boots, and you, my Hat,
Remain my friends: I feel, though I don't speak,
Your touch grow kindlier from week to week.
It well becomes our mutual happiness
To go toward the same end more or less.
There is not much dissimilarity,
Not much to choose, I know it well, in fine,
Between the purposes of you and me,
And your eventual Rubbish Heap, and mine.

Harold Monro

STRANGE MEETINGS

If suddenly a clod of earth should rise,
And walk about, and breathe, and speak, and love,
How one would tremble, and in what surprise
Gasp: " Can you move?"

I see men walking, and I always feel:
" Earth! How have you done this? What can
     you be?"
I can't learn how to know men, or conceal
How strange they are to me.

T. M. Kettle

Thomas M. Kettle was born at Artane County, Dublin, in 1880 and was educated at University College, where he won the Gold Medal for Oratory. His extraordinary faculty for grasping an intricate problem and crystallizing it in an epigram, or scoring his adversaries with one bright flash, was apparent even then. He was admitted to the bar in 1905 but soon abandoned the law to devote himself to journalism, which, because of his remarkable style, never remained journalism in his hands. In 1906 he entered politics; in 1910 he was re-elected for East Tyrone. Even his bitterest opponents conceded that Tom Kettle (as he was called by friend and enemy) was the most honorable of fighters; they acknowledged his honesty, courage and devotion to the cause of a United Ireland —and respected his penetrating wit. He once spoke of a Mr. Healy as " a brilliant calamity" and satirized a long-winded speaker by saying, " Mr. Long knows a sentence should have a beginning, but he quite forgets it should also have an end."

T. M. Kettle

"An Irish torch-bearer" (so E. B. Osborn calls him), Kettle fell in action at Ginchy, leading his Fusiliers in September, 1916. The uplifted poem to his daughter was written shortly before his death.

TO MY DAUGHTER BETTY, THE GIFT OF GOD

In wiser days, my darling rosebud, blown
To beauty proud as was your mother's prime,
In that desired, delayed, incredible time,
You'll ask why I abandoned you, my own,
And the dear heart that was your baby throne,
To dice with death. And oh! they'll give you
    rhyme
And reason: some will call the thing sublime,
And some decry it in a knowing tone.
So here, while the mad guns curse overhead,
And tired men sigh with mud for couch and floor,
Know that we fools, now with the foolish dead,
Died not for flag, nor King, nor Emperor,—
But for a dream, born in a herdsman's shed,
And for the secret Scripture of the poor.

Alfred Noyes

Alfred Noyes was born at Staffordshire, September 16, 1880. He is one of the few contemporary poets who have been fortunate enough to write a kind of poetry that is not only saleable but popular with many classes of people.

His first book, *The Loom of Years* (1902), was published when he was only 22 years old, and *Poems* (1904) intensified the promise of his first publication. Swinburne, grown old and living in retirement, was so struck with Noyes's talent that he had the young poet out to read to him. Unfortunately, Noyes has not developed his gifts as deeply as his admirers have hoped. His poetry, extremely straightforward and rhythmical, has often degenerated into cheap sentimentalities and cheaper tirades; it has frequently attempted to express programs and profundities far beyond Noyes's power.

What is most appealing about his best verse is its ease and heartiness; this singer's gift lies in the almost personal bond established between the poet and his public. People have such a good time reading his vivacious lines because Noyes had such a good time writing them. Rhyme in a thumping rhythm seems to be not merely his trade but his morning exercise. Noyes's own relish filled and quickened glees and catches like *Forty Singing Seamen* (1907), the lusty choruses in *Tales of the Mermaid Tavern* (1913), and the genuinely inspired nonsense of the earlier *Forest of Wild Thyme* (1905).

The least popular work of Noyes is, as a unified product, his most remarkable performance. It is an epic in twelve books of blank verse, *Drake* (1908), a glowing pageant of the sea and England's drama upon it. It is a spirited echo of the maritime Elizabethans; a vivid and orchestral work interspersed with splendid lyric passages and brisk songs. The companion volume, an attempted reconstruction of the literary phase of the same period, is less successful; but these *Tales of the Mermaid Tavern* (which introduce Shakespeare, Marlowe, Drayton, Raleigh, Ben Jonson, and other immortals) are alive and colorful, if somewhat too insistently rollicking and smoothly lilting.

His eight volumes were assembled in 1913 and published in two books of *Collected Poems* (Frederick A. Stokes Company).

SHERWOOD

Sherwood in the twilight, is Robin Hood awake?
Grey and ghostly shadows are gliding through the brake;
Shadows of the dappled deer, dreaming of the morn,
Dreaming of a shadowy man that winds a shadowy horn.

Alfred Noyes

Robin Hood is here again: all his merry thieves
Hear a ghostly bugle-note shivering through the leaves,
Calling as he used to call, faint and far away,
In Sherwood, in Sherwood, about the break of day.

Merry, merry England has kissed the lips of June:
All the wings of fairyland were here beneath the moon;
Like a flight of rose-leaves fluttering in a mist
Of opal and ruby and pearl and amethyst.

Merry, merry England is waking as of old,
With eyes of blither hazel and hair of brighter gold:
For Robin Hood is here again beneath the bursting spray
In Sherwood, in Sherwood, about the break of day.

Love is in the greenwood building him a house
Of wild rose and hawthorn and honeysuckle boughs;
Love it in the greenwood: dawn is in the skies;
And Marian is waiting with a glory in her eyes.

Hark! The dazzled laverock climbs the golden steep:
Marian is waiting: is Robin Hood asleep?
Round the fairy grass-rings frolic elf and fay,
In Sherwood, in Sherwood, about the break of day.

Oberon, Oberon, rake away the gold,
Rake away the red leaves, roll away the mould,
Rake away the gold leaves, roll away the red,
And wake Will Scarlett from his leafy forest bed.

Alfred Noyes

Friar Tuck and Little John are riding down together
With quarter-staff and drinking-can and grey goose-
    feather;
The dead are coming back again; the years are rolled
    away
In Sherwood, in Sherwood, about the break of day.

Softly over Sherwood the south wind blows;
All the heart of England hid in every rose
Hears across the greenwood the sunny whisper leap,
Sherwood in the red dawn, is Robin Hood asleep?

Hark, the voice of England wakes him as of old
And, shattering the silence with a cry of brighter gold,
Bugles in the greenwood echo from the steep,
Sherwood in the red dawn, is Robin Hood asleep?

Where the deer are gliding down the shadowy glen
All across the glades of fern he calls his merry men;
Doublets of the Lincoln green glancing through the May,
In Sherwood, in Sherwood, about the break of day;

Calls them and they answer: from aisles of oak and ash
Rings the *Follow! Follow!* and the boughs begin to
    crash;
The ferns begin to flutter and the flowers begin to fly;
And through the crimson dawning the robber band
    goes by.

Robin! Robin! Robin! All his merry thieves
Answer as the bugle-note shivers through the leaves:
Calling as he used to call, faint and far away,
In Sherwood, in Sherwood, about the break of day.

THE BARREL-ORGAN

There's a barrel-organ carolling across a golden street
   In the City as the sun sinks low;
And the music's not immortal; but the world has made
       it sweet
   And fulfilled it with the sunset glow;
And it pulses through the pleasures of the City and the
       pain
    That surround the singing organ like a large eternal
       light;
And they've given it a glory and a part to play again
   In the Symphony that rules the day and night.

And now it's marching onward through the realms of
       old romance,
   And trolling out a fond familiar tune,
And now it's roaring cannon down to fight the King of
       France,
   And now it's prattling softly to the moon.
And all around the organ there's a sea without a shore
   Of human joys and wonders and regrets;
To remember and to recompense the music evermore
   For what the cold machinery forgets . . .

Yes; as the music changes,
  Like a prismatic glass,
It takes the light and ranges
  Through all the moods that pass;
Dissects the common carnival
  Of passions and regrets,
And gives the world a glimpse of all
  The colours it forgets.

And there *La Traviata* sighs
  Another sadder song;
And there *Il Trovatore* cries
  A tale of deeper wrong;
And bolder knights to battle go
  With sword and shield and lance,
Than ever here on earth below
  Have whirled into—a dance!—

Go down to Kew in lilac-time, in lilac-time, in lilac-time;
  Go down to Kew in lilac-time (it isn't far from
    London!)
And you shall wander hand in hand with love in sum-
    mer's wonderland;
  Go down to Kew in lilac-time (it isn't far from
    London!)

The cherry-trees are seas of bloom and soft perfume and
    sweet perfume,
  The cherry-trees are seas of bloom (and oh, so near
    to London!)

And there they say, when dawn is high and all the world's
    a blaze of sky
  The cuckoo, though he's very shy, will sing a song
    for London.

The nightingale is rather rare and yet they say you'll
    hear him there
  At Kew, at Kew in lilac-time (and oh, so near to
    London!)
The linnet and the throstle, too, and after dark the long
    halloo
  And golden-eyed *tu-whit, tu-whoo* of owls that ogle
    London.

For Noah hardly knew a bird of any kind that isn't heard
  At Kew, at Kew in lilac-time (and oh, so near to
    London!)
And when the rose begins to pout and all the chestnut
    spires are out
  You'll hear the rest without a doubt, all chorusing
    for London:—

Come down to Kew in lilac-time, in lilac-time, in lilac-
    time;
  Come down to Kew in lilac-time (it isn't far from
    London!)
And you shall wander hand in hand with love in sum-
    mer's wonderland;
  Come down to Kew in lilac-time (is isn't far from
    London!)

156

And then the troubadour begins to thrill the golden
    street,
  In the city as the sun sinks low;
And in all the gaudy busses there are scores of weary
    feet
Marking time, sweet time, with a dull mechanic beat,
And a thousand hearts are plunging to a love they'll never
    meet,
Through the meadows of the sunset, through the poppies
    and the wheat,
  In the land where the dead dreams go.

Verdi, Verdi, when you wrote *Il Trovatore* did you
    dream
  Of the City when the sun sinks low,
Of the organ and the monkey and the many-coloured
    stream
On the Piccadilly pavement, of the myriad eyes that
    seem
To be litten for a moment with a wild Italian gleam
As *A che la morte* parodies the world's eternal theme
  And pulses with the sunset-glow?

There's a thief, perhaps, that listens with a face of frozen
    stone
  In the City as the sun sinks low;
There's a portly man of business with a balance of his
    own,
There's a clerk and there's a butcher of a soft reposeful
    tone,

And they're all of them returning to the heavens they
      have known:
They are crammed and jammed in busses and—they're
      each of them alone
   In the land where the dead dreams go.

There's a labourer that listens to the voices of the dead
   In the City as the sun sinks low;
And his hand begins to tremble and his face is rather red
As he sees a loafer watching him and—there he turns his
      head
And stares into the sunset where his April love is fled,
For he hears her softly singing and his lonely soul is led
   Through the land where the dead dreams go . . .

There's a barrel-organ carolling across a golden street
   In the City as the sun sinks low;
Though the music's only Verdi there's a world to make it
      sweet
Just as yonder yellow sunset where the earth and heaven
      meet
Mellows all the sooty City! Hark, a hundred thousand
      feet
Are marching on to glory through the poppies and the
      wheat
   In the land where the dead dreams go.

      So it's Jeremiah, Jeremiah,
        What have you to say
      When you meet the garland girls
        Tripping on their way?

Alfred Noyes

All around my gala hat
   I wear a wreath of roses
(A long and lonely year it is
   I've waited for the May!)
If any one should ask you,
   The reason why I wear it is—
My own love, my true love is coming
      home to-day.

And it's buy a bunch of violets for the lady
   (*It's lilac-time in London; it's lilac-time in London!*)
Buy a bunch of violets for the lady;
   While the sky burns blue above:

On the other side the street you'll find it shady
   (*It's lilac-time in London; it's lilac-time in London!*)
But buy a bunch of violets for the lady,
   And tell her she's your own true love.

There's a barrel-organ carolling across a golden
     street
   In the City as the sun sinks glittering and slow;
And the music's not immortal; but the world has made
     it sweet
And enriched it with the harmonies that make a song
     complete
In the deeper heavens of music where the night and morn-
     ing meet,
   As it dies into the sunset glow;

159

And it pulses through the pleasures of the City and the
  pain
That surround the singing organ like a large eternal
  light,
And they've given it a glory and a part to play again
  In the Symphony that rules the day and night.

And there, as the music changes,
  The song runs round again;
Once more it turns and ranges
  Through all its joy and pain:
Dissects the common carnival
  Of passions and regrets;
And the wheeling world remembers all
  The wheeling song forgets.

Once more *La Traviata* sighs
  Another sadder song:
Once more *Il Trovatore* cries
  A tale of deeper wrong;
Once more the knights to battle go
  With sword and shield and lance
Till once, once more, the shattered foe
  Has whirled into—a dance!

Come down to Kew in lilac-time, in lilac-time, in lilac-
  time;
  Come down to Kew in lilac-time (it isn't far from
    London!)

And you shall wander hand in hand with Love in sum-
    mer's wonderland,
Come down to Kew in lilac-time (it isn't far from
    London!)

EPILOGUE

(From " The Flower of Old Japan ")

Carol, every violet has
Heaven for a looking-glass!

Every little valley lies
Under many-clouded skies;
Every little cottage stands
Girt about with boundless lands.
Every little glimmering pond
Claims the mighty shores beyond—
Shores no seamen ever hailed,
Seas no ship has ever sailed.

All the shores when day is done
Fade into the setting sun,
So the story tries to teach
More than can be told in speech.

Beauty is a fading flower,
Truth is but a wizard's tower,
Where a solemn death-bell tolls,
And a forest round it rolls.

Alfred Noyes

We have come by curious ways
To the light that holds the days;
We have sought in haunts of fear
For that all-enfolding sphere:
And lo! it was not far, but near.
We have found, O foolish-fond,
The shore that has no shore beyond.

Deep in every heart it lies
With its untranscended skies;
For what heaven should bend above
Hearts that own the heaven of love?

Carol, Carol, we have come
Back to heaven, back to home.

Padraic Colum

Padraic Colum was born at Longford, Ireland (in the same county as Oliver Goldsmith), December 8, 1881, and was educated at the local schools. At 20 he was a member of a group that created the Irish National Theatre, afterwards called The Abbey Theatre.

Colum began as a dramatist with *Broken Soil* (1904), *The Land* (1905), *Thomas Muskerry* (1910), and this early dramatic influence has colored much of his work, his best poetry being in the form of dramatic lyrics. *Wild Earth,* his most notable collection of verse, first appeared in 1909, and an amplified edition of it was published in America in 1916.

THE PLOUGHER

Sunset and silence! A man: around him earth savage,
    earth broken;
Beside him two horses—a plough!

Earth savage, earth broken, the brutes, the dawn man
    there in the sunset,
And the Plough that is twin to the Sword, that is founder
    of cities!

"Brute-tamer, plough-maker, earth-breaker! Can'st
    hear?
  There are ages between us.
"Is it praying you are as you stand there alone in the
    sunset?

"Surely our sky-born gods can be naught to you, earth
    child and earth master?
"Surely your thoughts are of Pan, or of Wotan, or
    Dana?

"Yet, why give thought to the gods? Has Pan led your
    brutes where they stumble?
"Has Dana numbed pain of the child-bed, or Wotan put
    hands to your plough?

"What matter your foolish reply! O, man, standing
    lone and bowed earthward,
"Your task is a day near its close. Give thanks to the
    night-giving God."

  .   .   .   .

Slowly the darkness falls, the broken lands blend with
    the savage;
The brute-tamer stands by the brutes, a head's breadth
    only above them.

A head's breadth? Ay, but therein is hell's depth, and
    the height up to heaven,
And the thrones of the gods and their halls, their chariots,
    purples, and splendors.

AN OLD WOMAN OF THE ROADS

O, to have a little house!
To own the hearth and stool and all!
The heaped up sods upon the fire,
The pile of turf against the wall!

To have a clock with weights and chains
And pendulum swinging up and down!
A dresser filled with shining delph,
Speckled and white and blue and brown!

I could be busy all the day
Clearing and sweeping hearth and floor,
And fixing on their shelf again
My white and blue and speckled store!

I could be quiet there at night
Beside the fire and by myself,
Sure of a bed and loth to leave
The ticking clock and the shining delph!

Och! but I'm weary of mist and dark,
And roads where there's never a house nor bush,
And tired I am of bog and road,
And the crying wind and the lonesome hush!

Padraic Colum

And I am praying to God on high,
And I am praying Him night and day,
For a little house—a house of my own—
Out of the wind's and the rain's way.

Joseph Campbell

(Seosamh MacCathmhaoil)

Joseph Campbell was born in Belfast in 1881, and is not
only a poet but an artist; he made all the illustrations for *The
Rushlight* (1906), a volume of his own poems. Writing under
the Gaelic form of his name, he has published half a dozen
books of verse, the most striking of which is *The Mountainy
Singer,* first published in Dublin in 1909.

I AM THE MOUNTAINY SINGER

I am the mountainy singer—
The voice of the peasant's dream,
The cry of the wind on the wooded hill,
The leap of the fish in the stream.

Quiet and love I sing—
The carn on the mountain crest,
The *cailin* in her lover's arms,
The child at its mother's breast.

Beauty and peace I sing—
The fire on the open hearth,
The *cailleach* spinning at her wheel,
The plough in the broken earth.

165

Joseph Campbell

Travail and pain I sing—
The bride on the childing bed,
The dark man laboring at his rhymes,
The eye in the lambing shed.

Sorrow and death I sing—
The canker come on the corn,
The fisher lost in the mountain loch,
The cry at the mouth of morn.

No other life I sing,
For I am sprung of the stock
That broke the hilly land for bread,
And built the nest in the rock!

THE OLD WOMAN

As a white candle
   In a holy place,
So is the beauty
   Of an aged face.

As the spent radiance
   Of the winter sun,
So is a woman
   With her travail done,

Her brood gone from her,
   And her thoughts as still
As the waters
   Under a ruined mill.

James Stephens

This unique personality was born in Dublin in February, 1882. Stephens was discovered in an office and saved from clerical slavery by George Russell ("A. E."). Always a poet, Stephens's most poetic moments are in his highly-colored prose. And yet, although the finest of his novels, *The Crock of Gold* (1912), contains more wild phantasy and quaint imagery than all his volumes of verse, his *Insurrections* (1909) and *The Hill of Vision* (1912) reveal a rebellious spirit that is at once hotly ironic and coolly whimsical.

Stephens's outstanding characteristic is his delightful blend of incongruities—he combines in his verse the grotesque, the buoyant and the profound. No fresher or more brightly vigorous imagination has come out of Ireland since J. M. Synge.

THE SHELL

And then I pressed the shell
Close to my ear
And listened well,
And straightway like a bell
Came low and clear
The slow, sad murmur of the distant seas,
Whipped by an icy breeze
Upon a shore
Wind-swept and desolate.
It was a sunless strand that never bore
The footprint of a man,
Nor felt the weight
Since time began
Of any human quality or stir
Save what the dreary winds and waves incur.
And in the hush of waters was the sound
Of pebbles rolling round,
For ever rolling with a hollow sound.

And bubbling sea-weeds as the waters go
Swish to and fro
Their long, cold tentacles of slimy grey.
There was no day,
Nor ever came a night
Setting the stars alight
To wonder at the moon:
Was twilight only and the frightened croon,
Smitten to whimpers, of the dreary wind
And waves that journeyed blind—
And then I loosed my ear . . . O, it was sweet
To hear a cart go jolting down the street.

WHAT TOMAS AN BUILE SAID IN A PUB

I saw God. Do you doubt it?
   Do you dare to doubt it?
I saw the Almighty Man. His hand
Was resting on a mountain, and
He looked upon the World and all about it:
I saw him plainer than you see me now,
   You mustn't doubt it.

He was not satisfied;
   His look was all dissatisfied.
His beard swung on a wind far out of sight
Behind the world's curve, and there was light
Most fearful from His forehead, and He sighed,
" That star went always wrong, and from the start
   I was dissatisfied."

168

He lifted up His hand—
  I say He heaved a dreadful hand
Over the spinning Earth. Then I said, "Stay,
You must not strike it, God; I'm in the way;
And I will never move from where I stand."
He said, "Dear child, I feared that you were dead,"
  And stayed His hand.

TO THE FOUR COURTS, PLEASE

The driver rubbed at his nettly chin
With a huge, loose forefinger, crooked and black,
And his wobbly, violet lips sucked in,
And puffed out again and hung down slack:
One fang shone through his lop-sided smile,
In his little pouched eye flickered years of guile.

And the horse, poor beast, it was ribbed and forked,
And its ears hung down, and its eyes were old,
And its knees were knuckly, and as we talked
It swung the stiff neck that could scarcely hold
Its big, skinny head up—then I stepped in,
And the driver climbed to his seat with a grin.

God help the horse and the driver too,
And the people and beasts who have never a friend,
For the driver easily might have been you,
And the horse be me by a different end.
And nobody knows how their days will cease,
And the poor, when they're old, have little of peace.

John Drinkwater

Primarily a poetic dramatist, John Drinkwater, born in 1882, is best known as the author of *Abraham Lincoln—A Play* (1919) founded on Lord Charnwood's masterly and analytical biography. He has published several volumes of poems, most of them meditative and elegiac in mood.

The best of his verses have been collected in *Poems, 1908-19*, and the two here reprinted are used by permission, and by special arrangement with Houghton Mifflin Company, the authorized publishers.

RECIPROCITY

I do not think that skies and meadows are
Moral, or that the fixture of a star
Comes of a quiet spirit, or that trees
Have wisdom in their windless silences.
Yet these are things invested in my mood
With constancy, and peace, and fortitude;
That in my troubled season I can cry
Upon the wide composure of the sky,
And envy fields, and wish that I might be
As little daunted as a star or tree.

A TOWN WINDOW

Beyond my window in the night
　Is but a drab inglorious street,
Yet there the frost and clean starlight
　As over Warwick woods are sweet.

170

John Drinkwater

Under the grey drift of the town
  The crocus works among the mould
As eagerly as those that crown
  The Warwick spring in flame and gold.

And when the tramway down the hill
  Across the cobbles moans and rings,
There is about my window-sill
  The tumult of a thousand wings.

James Joyce

James Joyce was born at Dublin, February 2, 1882, and edu-
cated in Ireland. He is best known as a highly sensitive and
strikingly original writer of prose, his most celebrated works
being *Dubliners* (1914) and the novel, *A Portrait of the Artist
as a Young Man* (1916). His one volume of verse, *Chamber
Music,* was published in this country in 1918.

I HEAR AN ARMY

I hear an army charging upon the land,
  And the thunder of horses plunging, foam about their
      knees:
Arrogant, in black armour, behind them stand,
  Disdaining the reins, with fluttering whips, the
      charioteers.

They cry unto the night their battle-name:
  I moan in sleep when I hear afar their whirling
      laughter.
They cleave the gloom of dreams, a blinding flame,
  Clanging, clanging upon the heart as upon an anvil.

James Joyce

They come shaking in triumph their long, green hair:
  They come out of the sea and run shouting by the shore.
My heart, have you no wisdom thus to despair?
  My love, my love, my love, why have you left me alone?

J. C. Squire

Jack Collings Squire was born April 2, 1884, at Plymouth, of Devonian ancestry. He was educated at Blundell's and Cambridge University, and became known first as a remarkably adroit parodist. His *Imaginary Speeches* (1912) and *Tricks of the Trade* (1917) are amusing parodies and, what is more, excellent criticism. He edited *The New Statesman* for a while and founded *The London Mercury* (a monthly of which he is editor) in November, 1919. Under the pseudonym "Solomon Eagle" he wrote a page of literary criticism every week for six years, many of these papers being collected in his volume, *Books in General* (1919).

His original poetry is intellectual but simple, sometimes metaphysical and always interesting technically in its fluent and variable rhythms. A collection of his best verse up to 1919 was published under the title, *Poems: First Series*.

A HOUSE

Now very quietly, and rather mournfully,
  In clouds of hyacinth the sun retires,
And all the stubble-fields that were so warm to him
  Keep but in memory their borrowed fires.

And I, the traveller, break, still unsatisfied,
  From that faint exquisite celestial strand,
And turn and see again the only dwelling-place
  In this wide wilderness of darkening land.

172

J. C. Squire

The house, that house, O now what change has come
      to it.
  Its crude red-brick façade, its roof of slate;
What imperceptible swift hand has given it
  A new, a wonderful, a queenly state?

No hand has altered it, that parallelogram,
  So inharmonious, so ill-arranged;
That hard blue roof in shape and colour's what it
      was;
  No, it is not that any line has changed.

Only that loneliness is now accentuate
  And, as the dusk unveils the heaven's deep cave,
This small world's feebleness fills me with awe again,
  And all man's energies seem very brave.

And this mean edifice, which some dull architect
  Built for an ignorant earth-turning hind,
Takes on the quality of that magnificent
  Unshakable dauntlessness of human kind.

Darkness and stars will come, and long the night
      will be,
  Yet imperturbable that house will rest,
Avoiding gallantly the stars' chill scrutiny,
  Ignoring secrets in the midnight's breast.

Thunders may shudder it, and winds demoniac
  May howl their menaces, and hail descend:
Yet it will bear with them, serenely, steadfastly,
  Not even scornfully, and wait the end.

J. C. Squire

And all a universe of nameless messengers
　　From unknown distances may whisper fear,
And it will imitate immortal permanence,
　　And stare and stare ahead and scarcely hear.

It stood there yesterday; it will to-morrow, too,
　　When there is none to watch, no alien eyes
To watch its ugliness assume a majesty
　　From this great solitude of evening skies.

So lone, so very small, with worlds and worlds around,
　　While life remains to it prepared to outface
Whatever awful unconjectured mysteries
　　May hide and wait for it in time and space.

Lascelles Abercrombie

Lascelles Abercrombie was born in 1884. Like Masefield, he gained his reputation rapidly; totally unknown until 1909, upon the publication of *Interludes and Poems*, he was recognized as one of the greatest metaphysical poets of his period. *Emblems of Love* (1912), the ripest collection of his blank verse dialogues, justified the enthusiasm of his admirers.

Many of Abercrombie's poems, the best of which are too long to quote, are founded on scriptural themes, but his blank verse is not biblical either in mood or manner. It is the undercurrent rather than the surface of his verse which moves with a strong religious conviction. Abercrombie's images are daring and brilliant; his lines, sometimes too closely packed, glow with a dazzling intensity that is warmly spiritual and fervently human.

Lascelles Abercrombie

FROM "VASHTI"

What thing shall be held up to woman's beauty?
Where are the bounds of it? Yea, what is all
The world, but an awning scaffolded amid
The waste perilous Eternity, to lodge
This Heaven-wander'd princess, woman's beauty?
The East and West kneel down to thee, the
        North
And South; and all for thee their shoulders bear
The load of fourfold space. As yellow morn
Runs on the slippery waves of the spread sea,
Thy feet are on the griefs and joys of men
That sheen to be thy causey. Out of tears
Indeed, and blitheness, murder and lust and love,
Whatever has been passionate in clay,
Thy flesh was tempered. Behold in thy body
The yearnings of all men measured and told,
Insatiate endless agonies of desire
Given thy flesh, the meaning of thy shape!
What beauty is there, but thou makest it?
How is earth good to look on, woods and fields,
The season's garden, and the courageous hills,
All this green raft of earth moored in the seas?
The manner of the sun to ride the air,
The stars God has imagined for the night?
What's this behind them, that we cannot near,
Secret still on the point of being blabbed,

The ghost in the world that flies from being named?
Where do they get their beauty from, all these?
They do but glaze a lantern lit for man,
And woman's beauty is the flame therein.

SONG

(*From " Judith "*)

Balkis was in her marble town,
And shadow over the world came down.
Whiteness of walls, towers and piers,
That all day dazzled eyes to tears,
Turned from being white-golden flame,
And like the deep-sea blue became.
Balkis into her garden went;
Her spirit was in discontent
Like a torch in restless air.
Joylessly she wandered there,
And saw her city's azure white
Lying under the great night,
Beautiful as the memory
Of a worshipping world would be
In the mind of a god, in the hour
When he must kill his outward power;
And, coming to a pool where trees
Grew in double greeneries,
Saw herself, as she went by
The water, walking beautifully,

And saw the stars shine in the glance
Of her eyes, and her own fair countenance
Passing, pale and wonderful,
Across the night that filled the pool.
And cruel was the grief that played
With the queen's spirit; and she said:
"What do I here, reigning alone?
For to be unloved is to be alone.
There is no man in all my land
Dare my longing understand;
The whole folk like a peasant bows
Lest its look should meet my brows
And be harmed by this beauty of mine.
I burn their brains as I were sign
Of God's beautiful anger sent
To master them with punishment
Of beauty that must pour distress
On hearts grown dark with ugliness.
But it is I am the punisht one.
Is there no man, is there none,
In whom my beauty will but move
The lust of a delighted love;
In whom some spirit of God so thrives
That we may wed our lonely lives.
Is there no man, is there none?"—
She said, "I will go to Solomon."

James Elroy Flecker

Another remarkable poet whose early death was a blow to English literature, James Elroy Flecker, was born in London, November 5, 1884. Possibly due to his low vitality, Flecker found little to interest him but a classical reaction against realism in verse, a delight in verbal craftsmanship, and a passion for technical perfection—especially the deliberate technique of the French Parnassians whom he worshipped. Flecker was opposed to any art that was emotional or that "taught" anything. "The poet's business," he declared, "is not to save the soul of man, but to make it worth saving."

The advent of the war began to make Flecker's verse more personal and romantic. The tuberculosis that finally killed him at Davos Platz, Switzerland, January 3, 1915, forced him from an Olympian disinterest to a deep concern with life and death. He passionately denied that he was weary of living "as the pallid poets are," and he was attempting higher flights of song when his singing ceased altogether.

His two colorful volumes are *The Golden Journey to Samarkand* (1913) and *The Old Ships* (1915).

THE OLD SHIPS

I have seen old ships sail like swans asleep
Beyond the village which men still call Tyre,
With leaden age o'ercargoed, dipping deep
For Famagusta and the hidden sun
That rings black Cyprus with a lake of fire;
And all those ships were certainly so old—
Who knows how oft with squat and noisy gun,
Questing brown slaves or Syrian oranges,
The pirate Genoese
Hell-raked them till they rolled

178

James Elroy Flecker

Blood, water, fruit and corpses up the hold.
But now through friendly seas they softly run,
Painted the mid-sea blue or shore-sea green,
Still patterned with the vine and grapes in gold.

But I have seen,
Pointing her shapely shadows from the dawn
And image tumbled on a rose-swept bay,
A drowsy ship of some yet older day;
And, wonder's breath indrawn,
Thought I—who knows—who knows—but in that
    same
(Fished up beyond Aeaea, patched up new
—Stern painted brighter blue—)
That talkative, bald-headed seaman came
(Twelve patient comrades sweating at the oar)
From Troy's doom-crimson shore,
And with great lies about his wooden horse
Set the crew laughing, and forgot his course.

It was so old a ship—who knows, who knows?
—And yet so beautiful, I watched in vain
To see the mast burst open with a rose,
And the whole deck put on its leaves again.

D. H. Lawrence

David Herbert Lawrence, born in 1885, is one of the most
psychologically intense of the modern poets. This intensity,
ranging from a febrile morbidity to an exalted and almost
frenzied mysticism, is seen even in his prose works—particu-
larly in his short stories, *The Prussian Officer* (1917), his

analytical *Sons and Lovers* (1913), and the rhapsodic novel, *The Rainbow* (1915).

As a poet he is often caught in the net of his own emotions; his passion thickens his utterance and distorts his rhythms, which sometimes seem purposely harsh and bitter-flavored. But within his range he is as powerful as he is poignant. His most notable volumes of poetry are *Amores* (1916), *Look! We Have Come Through!* (1918), and *New Poems* (1920).

PEOPLE

The great gold apples of light
Hang from the street's long bough
    Dripping their light
On the faces that drift below,
On the faces that drift and blow
Down the night-time, out of sight
    In the wind's sad sough.

The ripeness of these apples of night
Distilling over me
    Makes sickening the white
Ghost-flux of faces that hie
Them endlessly, endlessly by
Without meaning or reason why
    They ever should be.

PIANO

Softly, in the dusk, a woman is singing to me;
Taking me back down the vista of years, till I see
A child sitting under the piano, in the boom of the
    tingling strings
And pressing the small, poised feet of a mother who
    smiles as she sings.

D. H. Lawrence

In spite of myself, the insidious mastery of song
Betrays me back, till the heart of me weeps to belong
To the old Sunday evenings at home, with winter
        outside
And hymns in the cosy parlour, the tinkling piano
        our guide.

So now it is vain for the singer to burst into clamour
With the great black piano appassionato. The glamour
Of childish days is upon me, my manhood is cast
Down in the flood of remembrance, I weep like a child
        for the past.

John Freeman

John Freeman, born in 1885, has published several volumes
of pleasantly descriptive verse. The two most distinctive are
Stone Trees (1916) and *Memories of Childhood* (1919).

STONE TREES

Last night a sword-light in the sky
Flashed a swift terror on the dark.
In that sharp light the fields did lie
Naked and stone-like; each tree stood
Like a tranced woman, bound and stark.
        Far off the wood
With darkness ridged the riven dark.

John Freeman

And cows astonished stared with fear,
And sheep crept to the knees of cows,
And conies to their burrows slid,
And rooks were still in rigid boughs,
And all things else were still or hid.
     From all the wood
Came but the owl's hoot, ghostly, clear.

In that cold trance the earth was held
It seemed an age, or time was nought.
Sure never from that stone-like field
Sprang golden corn, nor from those chill
Grey granite trees was music wrought.
     In all the wood
Even the tall poplar hung stone still.

It seemed an age, or time was none . . .
Slowly the earth heaved out of sleep
And shivered, and the trees of stone
Bent and sighed in the gusty wind,
And rain swept as birds flocking sweep.
     Far off the wood
Rolled the slow thunders on the wind.

From all the wood came no brave bird,
No song broke through the close-fall'n night,
Nor any sound from cowering herd:
Only a dog's long lonely howl
When from the window poured pale light.
     And from the wood
The hoot came ghostly of the owl.

Shane Leslie

Shane Leslie, the only surviving son of Sir John Leslie, was born at Swan Park, Monaghan, Ireland, in 1886 and was educated at Eton and the University of Paris. He worked for a time among the Irish poor and was deeply interested in the Celtic revival. During the greater part of a year he lectured in the United States, marrying an American, Marjorie Ide.

Leslie has been editor of *The Dublin Review* since 1916. He is the author of several volumes on Irish political matters as well as *The End of a Chapter* and *Verses in Peace and War*.

FLEET STREET

I never see the newsboys run
　　Amid the whirling street,
　　With swift untiring feet,
To cry the latest venture done,
But I expect one day to hear
　　Them cry the crack of doom
　　And risings from the tomb,
With great Archangel Michael near;
And see them running from the Fleet
　　As messengers of God,
　　With Heaven's tidings shod
About their brave unwearied feet.

THE PATER OF THE CANNON

Father of the thunder,
　　Flinger of the flame,
Searing stars asunder,
　　Hallowed be Thy Name!

183

Shane Leslie

By the sweet-sung quiring
  Sister bullets hum,
By our fiercest firing,
  May Thy Kingdom come!

By Thy strong apostle
  Of the Maxim gun,
By his pentecostal
  Flame, *Thy Will be done!*

Give us, Lord, good feeding
  To Thy battles sped—
Flesh, white grained and bleeding,
  Give for daily bread!

Frances Cornford

The daughter of Francis Darwin, third son of Charles Darwin, Mrs. Frances Macdonald Cornford, whose husband is a Fellow and Lecturer of Trinity College, was born in 1886. She has published three volumes of unaffected lyrical verse, the most recent of which, *Spring Morning*, was brought out by The Poetry Bookshop in 1915.

PREÉXISTENCE

I laid me down upon the shore
  And dreamed a little space;
I heard the great waves break and roar;
  The sun was on my face.

Frances Cornford

My idle hands and fingers brown
    Played with the pebbles grey;
The waves came up, the waves went down,
    Most thundering and gay.

The pebbles, they were smooth and round
    And warm upon my hands,
Like little people I had found
    Sitting among the sands.

The grains of sand so shining-small
    Soft through my fingers ran;
The sun shone down upon it all,
    And so my dream began:

How all of this had been before;
    How ages far away
I lay on some forgotten shore
    As here I lie to-day.

The waves came shining up the sands,
    As here to-day they shine;
And in my pre-pelasgian hands
    The sand was warm and fine.

I have forgotten whence I came,
    Or what my home might be,
Or by what strange and savage name
    I called that thundering sea.

185

Frances Cornford

I only know the sun shone down
　　As still it shines to-day,
And in my fingers long and brown
　　The little pebbles lay.

Anna Wickham

Anna Wickham, one of the most individual of the younger
women-poets, has published two distinctive volumes, *The Con-
templative Quarry* (1915) and *The Man with a Hammer*
(1916).

THE SINGER

If I had peace to sit and sing,
Then I could make a lovely thing;
But I am stung with goads and whips,
So I build songs like iron ships.

Let it be something for my song,
If it is sometimes swift and strong.

REALITY

Only a starveling singer seeks
The stuff of songs among the Greeks.
Juno is old,
Jove's loves are cold;
Tales over-told.

Anna Wickham

By a new risen Attic stream
A mortal singer dreamed a dream.
Fixed he not Fancy's habitation,
Nor set in bonds Imagination.
There are new waters, and a new Humanity.
For all old myths give us the dream to be.
We are outwearied with Persephone;
Rather than her, we'll sing Reality.

SONG

I was so chill, and overworn, and sad,
To be a lady was the only joy I had.
I walked the street as silent as a mouse,
Buying fine clothes, and fittings for the house.

But since I saw my love
I wear a simple dress,
And happily I move
Forgetting weariness.

Siegfried Sassoon

Siegfried Loraine Sassoon, the poet whom Masefield hailed as "one of England's most brilliant rising stars," was born September 8, 1886. He was educated at Marlborough and Clare College, Cambridge, and was a captain in the Royal Welsh Fusiliers. He fought three times in France, once in Palestine, winning the Military Cross for bringing in wounded on the battlefield.

187

Siegfried Sassoon

His poetry divides itself sharply in two moods—the lyric and the ironic. His early lilting poems were without significance or individuality. But with *The Old Huntsman* (1917) Sassoon found his own idiom, and became one of the leading younger poets upon the appearance of this striking volume. The first poem, a long monologue evidently inspired by Masefield, gave little evidence of what was to come. Immediately following it, however, came a series of war poems, undisguised in their tragedy and bitterness. Every line of these quivering stanzas bore the mark of a sensitive and outraged nature; there was scarcely a phrase that did not protest against the "glorification" and false glamour of war.

Counter-Attack appeared in 1918. In this volume Sassoon turned entirely from an ordered loveliness to the gigantic brutality of war. At heart a lyric idealist, the bloody years intensified and twisted his tenderness till what was stubborn and satiric in him forced its way to the top. In *Counter-Attack* Sassoon found his angry outlet. Most of these poems are choked with passion; many of them are torn out, roots and all, from the very core of an intense conviction; they rush on, not so much because of the poet's art but almost in spite of it. A suave utterance, a neatly-joined structure would be out of place and even inexcusable in poems like "The Rear-Guard," "To Any Dead Officer," "Does It Matter?"—verses that are composed of love, fever and indignation.

Can Sassoon see nothing glorious or uplifting in war? His friend, Robert Nichols, another poet and soldier, speaks for him in a preface. "Let no one ever," Nichols quotes Sassoon as saying, "from henceforth say one word in any way countenancing war. It is dangerous even to speak of how here and there the individual may gain some hardship of soul by it. For war is hell, and those who institute it are criminals. Were there even anything to say for it, it should not be said; for its spiritual disasters far outweigh any of its advantages. . . ." Nichols adds his approval to these sentences, saying, "For myself, this is the truth. War does not ennoble, it degrades."

Early in 1920 Sassoon visited America. At the same time he brought out his *Picture Show* (1920), a vigorous answer to those who feared that Sassoon had "written himself out" or had begun to burn away in his own fire. Had Rupert Brooke

lived, he might have written many of these lacerated but some-
how exalted lines. Sassoon's three volumes are the most vital
and unsparing records of the war we have had. They syn-
thesize in poetry what Barbusse's *Under Fire* spreads out in
panoramic prose.

TO VICTORY

Return to greet me, colours that were my joy,
Not in the woeful crimson of men slain,
But shining as a garden; come with the streaming
Banners of dawn and sundown after rain.

I want to fill my gaze with blue and silver,
Radiance through living roses, spires of green,
Rising in young-limbed copse and lovely wood,
Where the hueless wind passes and cries unseen.

I am not sad; only I long for lustre,—
Tired of the greys and browns and leafless ash.
I would have hours that move like a glitter of
        dancers,
Far from the angry guns that boom and flash.

Return, musical, gay with blossom and fleetness,
Days when my sight shall be clear and my heart
        rejoice;
Come from the sea with breadth of approaching
        brightness,
When the blithe wind laughs on the hills with
        uplifted voice.

Siegfried Sassoon

DREAMERS

Soldiers are citizens of death's gray land,
    Drawing no dividend from time's to-morrows.
In the great hour of destiny they stand,
    Each with his feuds, and jealousies, and sorrows.
Soldiers are sworn to action; they must win
    Some flaming, fatal climax with their lives.
Soldiers are dreamers; when the guns begin
    They think of firelit homes, clean beds, and wives.

I see them in foul dug-outs, gnawed by rats,
    And in the ruined trenches, lashed with rain,
Dreaming of things they did with balls and bats,
    And mocked by hopeless longing to regain
Bank-holidays, and picture shows, and spats,
    And going to the office in the train.

THE REAR-GUARD

Groping along the tunnel, step by step,
He winked his prying torch with patching glare
From side to side, and sniffed the unwholesome air.

Tins, boxes, bottles, shapes too vague to know,
A mirror smashed, the mattress from a bed;
And he, exploring fifty feet below
The rosy gloom of battle overhead.

190

Tripping, he grabbed the wall; saw someone lie
Humped at his feet, half-hidden by a rug,
And stooped to give the sleeper's arm a tug.
" I'm looking for headquarters." No reply.
" God blast your neck!" (For days he'd had no
    sleep.)
" Get up and guide me through this stinking place."
Savage, he kicked a soft, unanswering heap,
And flashed his beam across the livid face
Terribly glaring up, whose eyes yet wore
Agony dying hard ten days before;
And fists of fingers clutched a blackening wound.
Alone he staggered on until he found
Dawn's ghost that filtered down a shafted stair
To the dazed, muttering creatures underground
Who hear the boom of shells in muffled sound.
At last, with sweat of horror in his hair,
He climbed through darkness to the twilight air,
Unloading hell behind him step by step.

THRUSHES

Tossed on the glittering air they soar and skim,
Whose voices make the emptiness of light
A windy palace. Quavering from the brim
Of dawn, and bold with song at edge of night,
They clutch their leafy pinnacles and sing
Scornful of man, and from his toils aloof

Whose heart's a haunted woodland whispering;
Whose thoughts return on tempest-baffled wing;
Who hears the cry of God in everything,
And storms the gate of nothingness for proof.

AFTERMATH

Have you forgotten yet? . . .
For the world's events have rumbled on since those
    gagged days,
Like traffic checked a while at the crossing of city
    ways:
And the haunted gap in your mind has filled with
    thoughts that flow
Like clouds in the lit heavens of life; and you're a man
    reprieved to go,
Taking your peaceful share of Time, with joy to
    spare.
But the past is just the same,—and War's a bloody
    game. . . .
Have you forgotten yet? . . .
Look down, and swear by the slain of the War that you'll
    never forget.

Do you remember the dark months you held the sector at
    Mametz,—
The nights you watched and wired and dug and piled
    sandbags on parapets?

Siegfried Sassoon

Do you remember the rats; and the stench
Of corpses rotting in front of the front-line trench,—
And dawn coming, dirty-white, and chill with a hopeless
    rain?
Do you ever stop and ask, " Is it all going to happen
    again?"

Do you remember that hour of din before the attack,—
And the anger, the blind compassion that seized and shook
    you then
As you peered at the doomed and haggard faces of your
    men?
Do you remember the stretcher-cases lurching back
With dying eyes and lolling heads, those ashen-grey
Masks of the lads who once were keen and kind and gay?

Have you forgotten yet? . . .
Look up, and swear by the green of the Spring that you'll
    never forget.

Rupert Brooke

Possibly the most famous of the Georgians, Rupert Brooke, was born at Rugby in August, 1887, his father being assistant master at the school. As a youth, Brooke was keenly interested in all forms of athletics; playing cricket, football, tennis, and swimming as well as most professionals. He was six feet tall, his finely molded head topped with a crown of loose hair of lively brown; " a golden young Apollo," said Edward Thomas. Another friend of his wrote, " to look at, he was part of the youth of the world. He was one of the handsomest Englishmen of his time." His beauty overstressed somewhat his naturally romantic disposition; his early poems are a blend of delight in the splendor of actuality and disillusion in a loveliness that dies. The shadow of John Donne lies over his pages.

This occasional cynicism was purged, when after several years of travel (he had been to Germany, Italy and Honolulu) the war came, turning Brooke away from

> "A world grown old and cold and weary . . .
> And half men, and their dirty songs and dreary,
> And all the little emptiness of love."

Brooke enlisted with a relief that was like a rebirth; he sought a new energy in the struggle "where the worst friend and enemy is but Death." After seeing service in Belgium, 1914, he spent the following winter in a training-camp in Dorsetshire and sailed with the British Mediterranean Expeditionary Force in February, 1915, to take part in the unfortunate Dardenelles Campaign.

Brooke never reached his destination. He died of blood-poison at Skyros, April 23, 1915. His early death was one of England's great literary losses; Lascelles Abercrombie, W. W. Gibson (with both of whom he had been associated on the quarterly, *New Numbers*), Walter De la Mare, the Hon. Winston Spencer Churchill, and a host of others united to pay tribute to the most brilliant and passionate of the younger poets.

Brooke's sonnet-sequence, *1914* (from which "The Soldier" is taken), which, with prophetic irony, appeared a few weeks before his death, contains the accents of immortality. And "The Old Vicarage, Grantchester" (unfortunately too long to reprint in this volume), is fully as characteristic of the lighter and more playful side of Brooke's temperament. Both these phases are combined in "The Great Lover," of which Abercrombie has written, "It is life he loves, and not in any abstract sense, but all the infinite little familiar details of life, remembered and catalogued with delightful zest."

Rupert Brooke

THE GREAT LOVER [1]

I have been so great a lover: filled my days
So proudly with the splendour of Love's praise,
The pain, the calm, and the astonishment,
Desire illimitable, and still content,
And all dear names men use, to cheat despair,
For the perplexed and viewless streams that bear
Our hearts at random down the dark of life.
Now, ere the unthinking silence on that strife
Steals down, I would cheat drowsy Death so far,
My night shall be remembered for a star
That outshone all the suns of all men's days.
Shall I not crown them with immortal praise
Whom I have loved, who have given me, dared with me
High secrets, and in darkness knelt to see
The inenarrable godhead of delight?
Love is a flame;—we have beaconed the world's night.
A city:—and we have built it, these and I.
An emperor:—we have taught the world to die.
So, for their sakes I loved, ere I go hence,
And the high cause of Love's magnificence,
And to keep loyalties young, I'll write those names
Golden for ever, eagles, crying flames,
And set them as a banner, that men may know,
To dare the generations, burn, and blow
Out on the wind of Time, shining and streaming. . . .

[1] From *The Collected Poems of Rupert Brooke.* Copyright, 1915, by John Lane Company and reprinted by permission.

195

Rupert Brooke

These I have loved:
      White plates and cups, clean-gleaming,
Ringed with blue lines; and feathery, faery dust;
Wet roofs, beneath the lamp-light; the strong crust
Of friendly bread; and many-tasting food;
Rainbows; and the blue bitter smoke of wood;
And radiant raindrops couching in cool flowers;
And flowers themselves, that sway through sunny
      hours,
Dreaming of moths that drink them under the moon;
Then, the cool kindliness of sheets, that soon
Smooth away trouble; and the rough male kiss
Of blankets; grainy wood; live hair that is
Shining and free; blue-massing clouds; the keen
Unpassioned beauty of a great machine;
The benison of hot water; furs to touch;
The good smell of old clothes; and other such—
The comfortable smell of friendly fingers,
Hair's fragrance, and the musty reek that lingers
About dead leaves and last year's ferns. . . .
                  Dear names,
And thousand others throng to me! Royal flames;
Sweet water's dimpling laugh from tap or spring;
Holes in the ground; and voices that do sing:
Voices in laughter, too; and body's pain,
Soon turned to peace; and the deep-panting train;
Firm sands; the little dulling edge of foam
That browns and dwindles as the wave goes home;
And washen stones, gay for an hour; the cold
Graveness of iron; moist black earthen mould;

Rupert Brooke

Sleep; and high places; footprints in the dew;
And oaks; and brown horse-chestnuts, glossy-new;
And new-peeled sticks; and shining pools on grass;—
All these have been my loves. And these shall pass.
Whatever passes not, in the great hour,
Nor all my passion, all my prayers, have power
To hold them with me through the gate of Death.
They'll play deserter, turn with the traitor breath,
Break the high bond we made, and sell Love's trust
And sacramented covenant to the dust.
—Oh, never a doubt but, somewhere, I shall wake,
And give what's left of love again, and make
New friends, now strangers. . . .
                   But the best I've known,
Stays here, and changes, breaks, grows old, is blown
About the winds of the world, and fades from brains
Of living men, and dies.
                Nothing remains.

O dear my loves, O faithless, once again
This one last gift I give: that after men
Shall know, and later lovers, far-removed
Praise you, " All these were lovely "; say, " He loved."

Rupert Brooke

DUST [1]

When the white flame in us is gone,
    And we that lost the world's delight
Stiffen in darkness, left alone
    To crumble in our separate night;

When your swift hair is quiet in death,
    And through the lips corruption thrust
Has stilled the labour of my breath—
    When we are dust, when we are dust!—

Not dead, not undesirous yet,
    Still sentient, still unsatisfied,
We'll ride the air, and shine and flit,
    Around the places where we died,

And dance as dust before the sun,
    And light of foot, and unconfined,
Hurry from road to road, and run
    About the errands of the wind.

And every mote, on earth or air,
    Will speed and gleam, down later days,
And like a secret pilgrim fare
    By eager and invisible ways,

Rupert Brooke

Nor ever rest, nor ever lie,
   Till, beyond thinking, out of view,
One mote of all the dust that's I
   Shall meet one atom that was you.

Then in some garden hushed from wind,
   Warm in a sunset's afterglow,
The lovers in the flowers will find
   A sweet and strange unquiet grow

Upon the peace; and, past desiring,
   So high a beauty in the air,
And such a light, and such a quiring,
   And such a radiant ecstasy there,

They'll know not if it's fire, or dew,
   Or out of earth, or in the height,
Singing, or flame, or scent, or hue,
   Or two that pass, in light, to light,

Out of the garden higher, higher . . .
   But in that instant they shall learn
The shattering fury of our fire,
   And the weak passionless hearts will burn

And faint in that amazing glow,
   Until the darkness close above;
And they will know—poor fools, they'll
      know!—
   One moment, what it is to love.

Rupert Brooke

THE SOLDIER [1]

If I should die, think only this of me;
    That there's some corner of a foreign field
That is for ever England. There shall be
    In that rich earth a richer dust concealed;
A dust whom England bore, shaped, made aware,
    Gave, once, her flowers to love, her ways to roam,
A body of England's breathing English air,
    Washed by the rivers, blest by suns of home.

And think, this heart, all evil shed away,
    A pulse in the eternal mind, no less
        Gives somewhere back the thoughts by England
            given;
Her sights and sounds; dreams happy as her day;
    And laughter, learnt of friends; and gentleness,
        In hearts at peace, under an English heaven.

Winifred M. Letts

Winifred M. Letts was born in Ireland in 1887, and her early
work concerned itself almost entirely with the humor and pathos
found in her immediate surroundings. Her *Songs from Leinster*
(1913) is her most characteristic collection; a volume full of
the poetry of simple people and humble souls. Although she has
called herself " a back-door sort of bard," she is particularly
effective in the old ballad measure and in her quaint portrayal

[1] From *The Collected Poems of Rupert Brooke.* Copyright,
1915, by John Lane Company and reprinted by permission.

of Irish peasants rather than of Gaelic kings and pagan heroes.
She has also written three novels, five books for children, a
later volume of *Poems of the War* and, during the conflict,
served as a nurse at various base hospitals.

GRANDEUR

Poor Mary Byrne is dead,
   An' all the world may see
Where she lies upon her bed
   Just as fine as quality.

She lies there still and white,
   With candles either hand
That'll guard her through the night:
   Sure she never was so grand.

She holds her rosary,
   Her hands clasped on her breast.
Just as dacint as can be
   In the habit she's been dressed.

In life her hands were red
   With every sort of toil,
But they're white now she is dead,
   An' they've sorra mark of soil.

The neighbours come and go,
   They kneel to say a prayer,
I wish herself could know
   Of the way she's lyin' there.

Winifred M. Letts

It was work from morn till night,
  And hard she earned her bread:
But I'm thinking she's a right
  To be aisy now she's dead.

When other girls were gay,
  At wedding or at fair,
She'd be toiling all the day,
  Not a minyit could she spare.

An' no one missed her face,
  Or sought her in a crowd,
But to-day they throng the place
  Just to see her in her shroud.

The creature in her life
  Drew trouble with each breath;
She was just " poor Jim Byrne's wife "—
  But she's lovely in her death.

I wish the dead could see
  The splendour of a wake,
For it's proud herself would be
  Of the keening that they make.

Och! little Mary Byrne,
  You welcome every guest,
Is it now you take your turn
  To be merry with the rest?

I'm thinking you'd be glad,
  Though the angels make your bed,
Could you see the care we've had
  To respect you—now you're dead.

THE SPIRES OF OXFORD

I saw the spires of Oxford
  As I was passing by,
The grey spires of Oxford
  Against the pearl-grey sky.
My heart was with the Oxford men
  Who went abroad to die.

The years go fast in Oxford,
  The golden years and gay,
The hoary Colleges look down
  On careless boys at play.
But when the bugles sounded war
  They put their games away.

The left the peaceful river,
  The cricket-field, the quad,
The shaven lawns of Oxford,
  To seek a bloody sod—
They gave their merry youth away
  For country and for God.

Winifred M. Letts

God rest you, happy gentlemen,
   Who laid your good lives down,
Who took the khaki and the gun
   Instead of cap and gown.
God bring you to a fairer place
   Than even Oxford town.

Francis Brett Young

Francis Brett Young, who is a novelist as well as a poet, and who has been called, by *The Manchester Guardian*, " one of the promising evangelists of contemporary poetry," has written much that is both graceful and grave. There is music and a message in his lines that seem to have as their motto: " Trust in the true and fiery spirit of Man." Best known as a writer of prose, his most prominent works are *Marching on Tanga* and *The Crescent Moon*.

Brett Young's *Five Degrees South* (1917) and his *Poems 1916–18* (1919) contain the best of his verse.

LOCHANILAUN

This is the image of my last content:
My soul shall be a little lonely lake,
So hidden that no shadow of man may break
The folding of its mountain battlement;
Only the beautiful and innocent
Whiteness of sea-born cloud drooping to shake
Cool rain upon the reed-beds, or the wake
Of churned cloud in a howling wind's descent.

204

Francis Brett Young

For there shall be no terror in the night
When stars that I have loved are born in me,
And cloudy darkness I will hold most fair;
But this shall be the end of my delight:—
That you, my lovely one, may stoop and see
Your image in the mirrored beauty there.

F. S. Flint

Known chiefly as an authority on modern French poetry,
F. S. Flint has published several volumes of original imagist
poems, besides having translated works of Verhaeren and
Jean de Bosschere.

LONDON

London, my beautiful,
it is not the sunset
nor the pale green sky
shimmering through the curtain
of the silver birch,
nor the quietness;
it is not the hopping
of birds
upon the lawn,
nor the darkness
stealing over all things
that moves me.

205

F. S. Flint

But as the moon creeps slowly
over the tree-tops
among the stars,
I think of her
and the glow her passing
sheds on men.

London, my beautiful,
I will climb
into the branches
to the moonlit tree-tops,
that my blood may be cooled
by the wind.

Edith Sitwell

Edith Sitwell was born at Scarborough, in Yorkshire, and is the sister of the poets, Osbert and Sacheverell Sitwell. In 1914 she came to London and has devoted herself to literature ever since, having edited the various anthologies of *Wheels* since 1916. Her first book, *The Mother and Other Poems* (1915), contains some of her best work, although *Clowns' Houses* (1918) reveals a more piquant idiom and a sharper turn of mind.

THE WEB OF EROS

Within your magic web of hair, lies furled
The fire and splendour of the ancient world;
The dire gold of the comet's wind-blown hair;
The songs that turned to gold the evening air

Edith Sitwell

When all the stars of heaven sang for joy.
The flames that burnt the cloud-high city Troy.
The mænad fire of spring on the cold earth;
The myrrh-lit flame that gave both death and birth
To the soul Phœnix; and the star-bright shower
That came to Danaë in her brazen tower . . .
Within your magic web of hair lies furled
The fire and splendour of the ancient world.

INTERLUDE

Amid this hot green glowing gloom
A word falls with a raindrop's boom . . .

Like baskets of ripe fruit in air
The bird-songs seem, suspended where

Those goldfinches—the ripe warm lights
Peck slyly at them—take quick flights.

My feet are feathered like a bird
Among the shadows scarcely heard;

I bring you branches green with dew
And fruits that you may crown anew

Your whirring waspish-gilded hair
Amid this cornucopia—

Until your warm lips bear the stains
And bird-blood leap within your veins.

207

F. W. Harvey

Harvey was a lance-corporal in the English army and was in the German prison camp at Gütersloh when he wrote *The Bugler,* one of the isolated great poems written during the war. Much of his other verse is haphazard and journalistic, although *Gloucestershire Friends* contains several lines that glow with the colors of poetry.

THE BUGLER

God dreamed a man;
Then, having firmly shut
Life like a precious metal in his fist
Withdrew, His labour done. Thus did begin
Our various divinity and sin.
For some to ploughshares did the metal twist,
And others—dreaming empires—straightway cut
Crowns for their aching foreheads. Others beat
Long nails and heavy hammers for the feet
Of their forgotten Lord. (Who dares to boast
That he is guiltless?) Others coined it: most
Did with it—simply nothing. (Here again
Who cries his innocence?) Yet doth remain
Metal unmarred, to each man more or less,
Whereof to fashion perfect loveliness.

For me, I do but bear within my hand
(For sake of Him our Lord, now long forsaken)
A simple bugle such as may awaken
With one high morning note a drowsing man:
That wheresoe'er within my motherland
That sound may come, 'twill echo far and wide
Like pipes of battle calling up a clan,
Trumpeting men through beauty to God's side.

T. P. Cameron Wilson

"Tony" P. Cameron Wilson was born in South Devon in 1889 and was educated at Exeter and Oxford. He wrote one novel besides several articles under the pseudonym *Tipuca,* a euphonic combination of the first three initials of his name.

When the war broke out he was a teacher in a school at Hindhead, Surrey; and, after many months of gruelling conflict, he was given a captaincy. He was killed in action by a machine-gun bullet March 23, 1918, at the age of 29.

SPORTSMEN IN PARADISE

They left the fury of the fight,
 And they were very tired.
The gates of Heaven were open quite,
 Unguarded and unwired.
There was no sound of any gun,
 The land was still and green;
Wide hills lay silent in the sun,
 Blue valleys slept between.

They saw far-off a little wood
 Stand up against the sky.
Knee-deep in grass a great tree stood;
 Some lazy cows went by . . .
There were some rooks sailed overhead,
 And once a church-bell pealed.
"God! but it's England," someone said,
 "And there's a cricket-field!"

W. J. Turner

W. J. Turner was born in 1889 and, although little known until his appearance in *Georgian Poetry 1916-17*, has written no few delicate and fanciful poems. *The Hunter* (1916) and *The Dark Wind* (1918) both contain many verses as moving and musical as his splendid lines on "Death," a poem which is unfortunately too long to quote.

ROMANCE

When I was but thirteen or so
    I went into a golden land,
Chimborazo, Cotopaxi
    Took me by the hand.

My father died, my brother too,
    They passed like fleeting dreams,
I stood where Popocatapetl
    In the sunlight gleams.

I dimly heard the master's voice
    And boys far-off at play,—
Chimborazo, Cotopaxi
    Had stolen me away.

I walked in a great golden dream
    To and fro from school—
Shining Popocatapetl
    The dusty streets did rule.

I walked home with a gold dark boy
    And never a word I'd say,
Chimborazo, Cotopaxi
    Had taken my speech away.

W. J. Turner

I gazed entranced upon his face
　Fairer than any flower—
O shining Popocatapetl
　It was thy magic hour:

The houses, people, traffic seemed
　Thin fading dreams by day;
Chimborazo, Cotopaxi,
　They had stolen my soul away!

Patrick MacGill

Patrick MacGill was born in Donegal in 1890. He was the son of poverty-stricken peasants and, between the ages of 12 and 19, he worked as farm-servant, drainer, potato-digger, and navvy, becoming one of the thousands of stray "tramp-laborers" who cross each summer from Ireland to Scotland to help gather in the crops. Out of his bitter experiences and the evils of modern industrial life, he wrote several vivid novels (*The Rat Pit* is an unforgettable document) and the tragedy-crammed *Songs of the Dead End.* He joined the editorial staff of *The Daily Express* in 1911; was in the British army during the war; was wounded at Loos in 1915; and wrote his *Soldier Songs* during the conflict.

BY-THE-WAY

These be the little verses, rough and uncultured, which
I've written in hut and model, deep in the dirty ditch,
On the upturned hod by the palace made for the idle rich.

211

Out on the happy highway, or lines where the engines go,
Which fact you may hardly credit, still for your doubts
  'tis so,
For I am the person who wrote them, and surely to God,
  I know!

Wrote them beside the hot-plate, or under the chilling
  skies,
Some of them true as death is, some of them merely lies,
Some of them very foolish, some of them otherwise.

Little sorrows and hopings, little and rugged rhymes,
Some of them maybe distasteful to the moral men of our
  times,
Some of them marked against me in the Book of the
  Many Crimes.

These, the Songs of a Navvy, bearing the taint of the
  brute,
Unasked, uncouth, unworthy out to the world I put,
Stamped with the brand of labor, the heel of a navvy's
  boot.

DEATH AND THE FAIRIES

Before I joined the Army
  I lived in Donegal,
Where every night the Fairies
  Would hold their carnival.

Patrick MacGill

But now I'm out in Flanders,
  Where men like wheat-ears fall,
And it's Death and not the Fairies
  Who is holding carnival.

Francis Ledwidge

Francis Ledwidge was born in Slane, County Meath, Ireland,
in 1891. His brief life was fitful and romantic. He was, at
various times, a miner, a grocer's clerk, a farmer, a scavenger,
an experimenter in hypnotism, and, at the end, a soldier. He
served as a lance-corporal on the Flanders front and was
killed in July, 1917, at the age of 26 years.

Ledwidge's poetry is rich in nature imagery; his lines are
full of color, in the manner of Keats, and unaffectedly melo-
dious.

AN EVENING IN ENGLAND

From its blue vase the rose of evening drops;
Upon the streams its petals float away.
The hills all blue with distance hide their tops
In the dim silence falling on the grey.
A little wind said " Hush!" and shook a spray
Heavy with May's white crop of opening bloom;
A silent bat went dipping in the gloom.

Night tells her rosary of stars full soon,
They drop from out her dark hand to her knees.
Upon a silhouette of woods, the moon

213

Leans on one horn as if beseeching ease
From all her changes which have stirred the seas.
Across the ears of Toil, Rest throws her veil.
I and a marsh bird only make a wail.

EVENING CLOUDS

A little flock of clouds go down to rest
In some blue corner off the moon's highway,
With shepherd-winds that shook them in the West
To borrowed shapes of earth, in bright array,
Perhaps to weave a rainbow's gay festoons
Around the lonesome isle which Brooke has made
A little England full of lovely noons,
Or dot it with his country's mountain shade.

Ah, little wanderers, when you reach that isle [1]
Tell him, with dripping dew, they have not failed,
What he loved most; for late I roamed a while
Thro' English fields and down her rivers sailed;
And they remember him with beauty caught
From old desires of Oriental Spring
Heard in his heart with singing overwrought;
And still on Purley Common gooseboys sing.

[1] The island of Skyros where Rupert Brooke was buried. (See
page 194.)

214

Richard Aldington

Alas, how poor the gifts that lovers give—
I can but give you of my flesh and strength,
I can but give you these few passing days
And passionate words that, since our speech began,
All lovers whisper in all ladies' ears.

I try to think of some one lovely gift
No lover yet in all the world has found;
I think: If the cold sombre gods
Were hot with love as I am
Could they not endow you with a star
And fix bright youth for ever in your limbs?
Could they not give you all things that I lack?

You should have loved a god; I am but dust.
Yet no god loves as loves this poor frail dust.

IMAGES

I

Like a gondola of green scented fruits
Drifting along the dank canals of Venice,
You, O exquisite one,
Have entered into my desolate city.

II

The blue smoke leaps
Like swirling clouds of birds vanishing.
So my love leaps forth toward you,
Vanishes and is renewed.

III

A rose-yellow moon in a pale sky
When the sunset is faint vermilion
In the mist among the tree-boughs
Art thou to me, my beloved.

IV

A young beech tree on the edge of the forest
Stands still in the evening,
Yet shudders through all its leaves in the
    light air
And seems to fear the stars—
So are you still and so tremble.

V

The red deer are high on the mountain,
They are beyond the last pine trees.
And my desires have run with them.

VI

The flower which the wind has shaken
Is soon filled again with rain;
So does my heart fill slowly with tears,
O Foam-Driver, Wind-of-the-Vineyards,
Until you return.

AT THE BRITISH MUSEUM

I turn the page and read:
" I dream of silent verses where the rhyme
Glides noiseless as an oar."

Richard Aldington

The heavy musty air, the black desks,
The bent heads and the rustling noises
In the great dome
Vanish . . .
And
The sun hangs in the cobalt-blue sky,
The boat drifts over the lake shallows,
The fishes skim like umber shades through the
    undulating weeds,
The oleanders drop their rosy petals on the lawns,
And the swallows dive and swirl and whistle
About the cleft battlements of Can Grande's
    castle. . . .

Edward Shanks

Edward Shanks was born in London in 1892 and educated at Trinity College, Cambridge. He has reviewed verse and *belles lettres* for several years for various English publications, and is at present assistant editor of *The London Mercury*. His *The Queen of China and Other Poems* appeared late in 1919.

COMPLAINT

When in the mines of dark and silent thought
Sometimes I delve and find strange fancies there,
With heavy labour to the surface brought
That lie and mock me in the brighter air,
Poor ores from starvèd lodes of poverty,
Unfit for working or to be refined,
That in the darkness cheat the miner's eye,
I turn away from that base cave, the mind.

219

Edward Shanks

Yet had I but the power to crush the stone
There are strange metals hid in flakes therein,
Each flake a spark sole-hidden and alone,
That only cunning, toilsome chemists win.
All this I know, and yet my chemistry
Fails and the pregnant treasures useless lie.

Osbert Sitwell

Born in London, December 6th, 1892, Osbert Sitwell (son of
Sir George Sitwell and brother of Edith Sitwell) was edu-
cated at Eton and became an officer in the Grenadier Guards,
with whom he served in France for various periods from 1914
to 1917.

His first contributions appeared in *Wheels* (an annual
anthology of a few of the younger radical writers, edited by
his sister) and disclosed an ironic and strongly individual
touch. That impression is strengthened by a reading of
Argonaut and Juggernaut (1920), where Sitwell's cleverness
and satire are fused. His most remarkable though his least
brilliant poems are his irregular and fiery protests against
smugness and hypocrisy. But even Sitwell's more conventional
poetry has a freshness of movement and definiteness of outline.

THE BLIND PEDLAR

I stand alone through each long day
Upon these pavers; cannot see
The wares spread out upon this tray
—For God has taken sight from me!

Osbert Sitwell

Many a time I've cursed the night
When I was born. My peering eyes
Have sought for but one ray of light
To pierce the darkness. When the skies

Rain down their first sweet April showers
On budding branches; when the morn
Is sweet with breath of spring and flowers,
I've cursed the night when I was born.

But now I thank God, and am glad
For what I cannot see this day
—The young men cripples, old, and sad,
With faces burnt and torn away;

Or those who, growing rich and old,
Have battened on the slaughter,
Whose faces, gorged with blood and gold,
Are creased in purple laughter!

PROGRESS

The city's heat is like a leaden pall—
Its lowered lamps glow in the midnight air
Like mammoth orange-moths that flit and flare
Through the dark tapestry of night. The tall
Black houses crush the creeping beggars down,
Who walk beneath and think of breezes cool,
Of silver bodies bathing in a pool;

Osbert Sitwell

Or trees that whisper in some far, small town
Whose quiet nursed them, when they thought that
Was merely metal, not a grave of mould
In which men bury all that's fine and fair.
When they could chase the jewelled butterfly
Through the green bracken-scented lanes or sigh
For all the future held so rich and rare;
When, though they knew it not, their baby cries
Were lovely as the jewelled butterflies.

Robert Nichols

Robert Nichols was born on the Isle of Wight in 1893. His
first volume, *Invocations* (1915), was published while he was
at the front, Nichols having joined the army while he was still
an undergraduate at Trinity College, Oxford. After serving
one year as second lieutenant in the Royal Field Artillery, he
was incapacitated by shell shock, visiting America in 1918-19
as a lecturer. His *Ardours and Endurances* (1917) is the most
representative work of this poet, although his new volume,
The Flower of Flame (1920), shows a steady advance in
power.

NEARER

Nearer and ever nearer . . .
My body, tired but tense,
Hovers 'twixt vague pleasure
And tremulous confidence.

Arms to have and to use them
And a soul to be made
Worthy, if not worthy;
If afraid, unafraid.

Robert Nichols

To endure for a little,
To endure and have done:
Men I love about me,
Over me the sun!

And should at last suddenly
Fly the speeding death,
The four great quarters of heaven
Receive this little breath.

Charles Hamilton Sorley

Charles Hamilton Sorley, who promised greater things than
any of the younger poets, was born at Old Aberdeen in May,
1895. He studied at Marlborough College and University
College, Oxford. He was finishing his studies abroad and was
on a walking-tour along the banks of the Moselle when the
war came. Sorley returned home to receive an immediate com-
mission in the 7th Battalion of the Suffolk Regiment. In Au-
gust, 1915, at the age of 20, he was made a captain. On Octo-
ber 13, 1915, he was killed in action near Hulluch.

Sorley left but one book, *Marlborough and Other Poems*. The
verse contained in it is sometimes rough but never rude. Al-
though he admired Masefield, loveliness rather than liveliness
was his aim. Restraint, tolerance, and a dignity unusual for a
boy of 20, distinguish his poetry.

TWO SONNETS

I

Saints have adored the lofty soul of you.
Poets have whitened at your high renown.
We stand among the many millions who
Do hourly wait to pass your pathway down.

223

You, so familiar, once were strange: we tried
To live as of your presence unaware.
But now in every road on every side
We see your straight and steadfast signpost there.

I think it like that signpost in my land
Hoary and tall, which pointed me to go
Upward, into the hills, on the right hand,
Where the mists swim and the winds shriek and
    blow,
A homeless land and friendless, but a land
I did not know and that I wished to know.

II

Such, such is Death: no triumph: no defeat:
Only an empty pail, a slate rubbed clean,
A merciful putting away of what has been.

And this we know: Death is not Life effete,
Life crushed, the broken pail. We who have seen
So marvellous things know well the end not yet.

Victor and vanquished are a-one in death:
Coward and brave: friend, foe. Ghosts do not say,
"Come, what was your record when you drew
    breath?"
But a big blot has hid each yesterday
So poor, so manifestly incomplete.
And your bright Promise, withered long and sped,
Is touched; stirs, rises, opens and grows sweet
And blossoms and is you, when you are dead.

Charles Hamilton Sorley

TO GERMANY

You are blind like us. Your hurt no man designed,
And no man claimed the conquest of your land.
But gropers both, through fields of thought confined,
We stumble and we do not understand.
You only saw your future bigly planned,
And we the tapering paths of our own mind,
And in each other's dearest ways we stand,
And hiss and hate. And the blind fight the blind.

When it is peace, then we may view again
With new-won eyes each other's truer form
And wonder. Grown more loving-kind and warm
We'll grasp firm hands and laugh at the old pain,
When it is peace. But until peace, the storm,
The darkness and the thunder and the rain.

Robert Graves

Robert Graves was born July 26, 1895. One of "the three
rhyming musketeers" (the other two being the poets Siegfried
Sassoon and Robert Nichols), he was one of several writers
who, roused by the war and giving himself to his country,
refused to glorify warfare or chant new hymns of hate. Like
Sassoon, Graves also reacts against the storm of fury and
blood-lust (see his poem "To a Dead Boche"), but, fortified
by a lighter and more whimsical spirit, where Sassoon is vio-
lent, Graves is volatile; where Sassoon is bitter, Graves is
almost blithe.

An unconquerable gayety rises from his *Fairies and Fusiliers*
(1917), a surprising and healing humor that is warmly indi-

225

Robert Graves

vidual. In *Country Sentiment* (1919) Graves turns to a fresh
and more serious simplicity. But a buoyant fancy ripples be-
neath the most archaic of his ballads and a quaintly original
turn of mind saves them from their own echoes.

IT'S A QUEER TIME

It's hard to know if you're alive or dead
When steel and fire go roaring through your head.

One moment you'll be crouching at your gun
Traversing, mowing heaps down half in fun:
The next, you choke and clutch at your right breast—
No time to think—leave all—and off you go . . .
To Treasure Island where the Spice winds blow,
To lovely groves of mango, quince and lime—
Breathe no good-bye, but ho, for the Red West!
        It's a queer time.

You're charging madly at them yelling " Fag! "
When somehow something gives and your feet drag.
You fall and strike your head; yet feel no pain
And find . . . you're digging tunnels through the
        hay
In the Big Barn, 'cause it's a rainy day.
Oh, springy hay, and lovely beams to climb!
You're back in the old sailor suit again.
        It's a queer time.

Or you'll be dozing safe in your dug-out—
A great roar—the trench shakes and falls about—
You're struggling, gasping, struggling, then . . .
　　　hullo!
Elsie comes tripping gaily down the trench,
Hanky to nose—that lyddite makes a stench—
Getting her pinafore all over grime.
Funny! because she died ten years ago!
　　　It's a queer time.

The trouble is, things happen much too quick;
Up jump the Boches, rifles thump and click,
You stagger, and the whole scene fades away:
Even good Christians don't like passing straight
From Tipperary or their Hymn of Hate
To Alleluiah-chanting, and the chime
Of golden harps . . . and . . . I'm not well
　　　to-day . . .
　　　It's a queer time.

A PINCH OF SALT

When a dream is born in you
　　With a sudden clamorous pain,
When you know the dream is true
　　And lovely, with no flaw nor stain,
O then, be careful, or with sudden clutch
You'll hurt the delicate thing you prize so much.

227

Dreams are like a bird that mocks,
  Flirting the feathers of his tail.
When you seize at the salt-box,
  Over the hedge you'll see him sail.
Old birds are neither caught with salt nor chaff:
They watch you from the apple bough and laugh.

Poet, never chase the dream.
  Laugh yourself, and turn away.
Mask your hunger; let it seem
  Small matter if he come or stay;
But when he nestles in your hand at last,
Close up your fingers tight and hold him fast.

I WONDER WHAT IT FEELS LIKE TO BE DROWNED?

Look at my knees,
That island rising from the steamy seas!
The candle's a tall lightship; my two hands
Are boats and barges anchored to the sands,
With mighty cliffs all round;
They're full of wine and riches from far lands. . . .
I wonder what it feels like to be drowned?

I can make caves,
By lifting up the island and huge waves
And storms, and then with head and ears well under
Blow bubbles with a monstrous roar like thunder,

A bull-of-Bashan sound.
The seas run high and the boats split asunder . . .
I wonder what it feels like to be drowned?

The thin soap slips
And slithers like a shark under the ships.
My toes. are on the soap-dish—that's the effect
Of my huge storms; an iron steamer's wrecked.
The soap slides round and round;
He's biting the old sailors, I expect. . . .
I wonder what it feels like to be drowned?

THE LAST POST

The bugler sent a call of high romance—
"Lights out! Lights out!" to the deserted square.
On the thin brazen notes he threw a prayer:
"God, if it's *this* for me next time in France,
O spare the phantom bugle as I lie
Dead in the gas and smoke and roar of guns,
Dead in a row with other broken ones,
Lying so stiff and still under the sky—
Jolly young Fusiliers, too good to die . . ."
The music ceased, and the red sunset flare
Was blood about his head as he stood there.

INDEX

231

Index

Index

233

Index

Printed in the United States
20459LVS00001B/46